CRIME SCENE INVESTIGATIONS CRIME SCENE INVESTIGATIONS CRIM

DNA Evidence
The Proof Is in the Genes

W9-DBD-379

By Cecilia Jennings

Portions of this book originally appeared in
DNA Evidence by Don Nardo.

DISCARD

LUCENT
PRESS

Published in 2018 by
Lucent Press, an Imprint of Greenhaven Publishing, LLC
353 3rd Avenue
Suite 255
New York, NY 10010

Designer: Deanna Paternostro
Editor: Jennifer Lombardo

Library of Congress Cataloging-in-Publication Data

Names: Jennings, Cecilia, author.
Title: DNA evidence : the proof is in the genes / Cecilia Jennings.
Description: New York : Lucent Press, [2018] | Series: Crime scene
  investigations | Includes bibliographical references and index.
Identifiers: LCCN 2017044918| ISBN 9781534561762 (library bound book) | ISBN
  9781534562738 (paperback book) | ISBN 9781534561755 (eBook)
Subjects: LCSH: DNA fingerprinting. | DNA–Analysis. | Forensic
  genetics–Technique. | Evidence, Criminal.
Classification: LCC RA1057.55 .J46 2018 | DDC 614/.1–dc23
LC record available at https://lccn.loc.gov/2017044918

Printed in the United States of America

CPSIA compliance information: Batch #CW18KL: For further information contact Greenhaven Publishing LLC, New York, New York at 1-844-317-7404.

Please visit our website, www.greenhavenpublishing.com. For a free color catalog of all our high-quality books, call toll free 1-844-317-7404 or fax 1-844-317-7405.

Contents

Foreword

For decades, popular television programs and movies have depicted the life and work of police officers, detectives, and crime scene investigators. Many of these shows and films portray forensic scientists as the brains responsible for cracking cases and bringing criminals to justice. Undoubtedly, these crime scene analysts are an important part in the process of crime solving. With modern technology and advances in forensic analysis, these highly trained experts are a crucial component of law enforcement systems all across the world.

Police officers and detectives are also integral members of the law enforcement team. They are the ones who respond to 911 calls about crime, collect physical evidence, and use their high level of training to identify suspects and culprits. They work right alongside forensic investigators to figure out the mysteries behind why a crime is committed, and the entire team cooperates to gather enough evidence to convict someone in a court of law.

Ever since the first laws were recorded, crime scene investigation has been handled in roughly the same way. An authority is informed that a crime has been committed; someone looks around the crime scene and interviews potential witnesses; suspects are identified based on evidence and testimony; and, finally, someone is formally accused of committing a crime. This basic plan is generally effective, and criminals are often caught and brought to justice. Throughout history, however, certain limitations have sometimes prevented authorities from finding out who was responsible for a crime.

There are many reasons why a crime goes unsolved: Maybe a dead body was found too late, evidence was tampered with, or witnesses lied. Sometimes, even the greatest technology of the age is simply not good enough to process and analyze the evidence at a crime scene. In the United States during the 20th century, for example, the person responsible for the infamous Zodiac killings was never found, despite the earnest efforts of hundreds of policemen, detectives, and forensic analysts.

In modern times, science and technology are integral to the investigative process. From DNA analysis to high-definition surveillance video, it has become much more difficult to commit a crime and get away with it. Using advanced computers and immense databases, microscopic skin cells from a crime scene can be collected and then analyzed by a forensic scientist, leading detectives to the home of the culprit of a crime. Dozens of people work behind the scenes of criminal investigations to figure out the unique and complex elements of a crime. Although this process is still time-consuming and complicated, technology is constantly improving and adapting to the needs of police forces worldwide.

This series is designed to help young readers understand the systems in place to allow forensic professionals to do their jobs. Covering a wide range of topics, from the assassination of President John F. Kennedy to 21st-century cybercriminals, these titles describe in detail the ways in which technology and criminal investigations have evolved over more than 50 years. They cite eyewitnesses and experts in order to give a detailed and nuanced picture of the difficult task of rooting out criminals. Although television shows and movies add drama to the crime scene investigation process, these real-life stories have enough drama on their own. This series sticks to the facts surrounding some of the highest-profile criminal cases of the modern era and the people who work to solve them and other crimes every day.

Introduction
Crime Scene Science

Although crime-solving work is a lot more than simply matching suspects to deoxyribonucleic acid (DNA), it is true that DNA can be useful to detectives when they are trying to prove someone's involvement in a crime. Because DNA is unique in every individual, it can be thought of as the genetic blueprint of humans and other living things—indeed, DNA is sometimes referred to as the "genetic fingerprint." Just like someone's fingerprints can prove that they touched or handled a certain object, DNA can be used to place a suspect at the scene of a crime—or prove they were not there. This process is sometimes called DNA fingerprinting, even though it does not involve actual fingerprints. More commonly, it is called DNA analysis.

Modern television crime dramas have helped make the public aware that DNA analysis is part of a special branch of science called forensic science, often simply called "forensics." Forensics applies scientific methods to legal matters, particularly to solving crimes. DNA is not the only form of evidence used in the fascinating world of forensic science. The forensic experts depicted on *CSI: Crime Scene Investigation*, often referred to as just *CSI*, and other shows regularly supplement their DNA analysis by examining finger and palm prints, shoe and tire tracks, blood types, cloth fibers, and many other kinds of forensic evidence.

The Long History of Forensic Science

The use of DNA analysis as a scientific crime-solving technique became available to law enforcement officials only in the last few decades, as technology evolved to allow investigators to collect and analyze samples left behind at crime scenes. The forensic use of DNA is the result of a long, winding, often uneven history of scientific crime solving. Like all areas of scientific inquiry, DNA's use in criminal investigations would not have happened without many years of study. In fact, widespread understanding of forensic methods did not exist until about a century ago. However, police and other investigators have attempted to solve crimes throughout recorded human history, and basic scientific techniques—although not yet called "science" or "forensics"—were introduced into the process a little at a time over the centuries.

The first known use of forensics to solve a murder case occurred in China, sometime before 1248. This is known thanks to Chinese writer Song Ci, who compiled a book titled *Collected Cases of Injustice Rectified*. The volume told about various investigations by doctors and other authorities into people's deaths to make sure justice had been

The Chinese were the first known people to use forensics. The case involved a man who had been murdered with a sickle similar to the one shown here.

served. In one important case, a man had been murdered with a farm tool called a sickle. In an effort to find the guilty party, the investigator asked each villager who owned a sickle to bring it to him. After a while, flies began to gather on one particular sickle. The investigator reasoned that the flies were attracted to traces of blood left on the blade after the killer had wiped it off. They were able to get a confession from the sickle's owner and thereby solve the murder. Today, an investigator might conduct an investigation much the same way, but rather than using flies, they would test each blade for traces of DNA and compare them to the DNA of the victim.

The Rise of Crime Scene Detectives

Centuries after Song Ci reported on the use of flies to detect blood residue, various other forensic techniques began to develop in Europe. An early example is the 1816 murder of a young woman in Warwick, England. A police investigator found grains of wheat, boot prints, and the impression of a certain kind of cloth in the soft earth near the body. He then matched these impressions with the trousers of a farm laborer who lived nearby and had been threshing the wheat near the crime scene, solving the case. The investigator's careful examination of the crime scene allowed him to spot key pieces of evidence the killer had

left behind—much the way that, centuries later, police and forensic scientists would analyze a crime scene for traces of DNA.

Inspired by early investigators, in the mid-1800s, a young English doctor named Alfred Swaine Taylor began teaching forensic medicine in London, England. He was the first researcher to support a careful examination of all evidence at a crime scene by a trained medical expert. In a way, this marked the birth of the modern crime scene investigator (CSI). Taylor wrote,

A medical man, when he sees a dead body, should notice everything. He should observe everything which could throw a light on the production of wounds or other injuries found upon it. It should not be left to a policeman to say whether there were any marks of blood on the dress or on the hands of the deceased, or on the furniture of the room. The dress of the deceased as well as the body should always be closely examined on the spot by a medical man.[1]

The "medical man" Taylor mentioned is a combination of today's medical examiner and CSI unit. It is the CSI unit's job to meticulously, or carefully, document everything at the scene, take samples of anything they think might

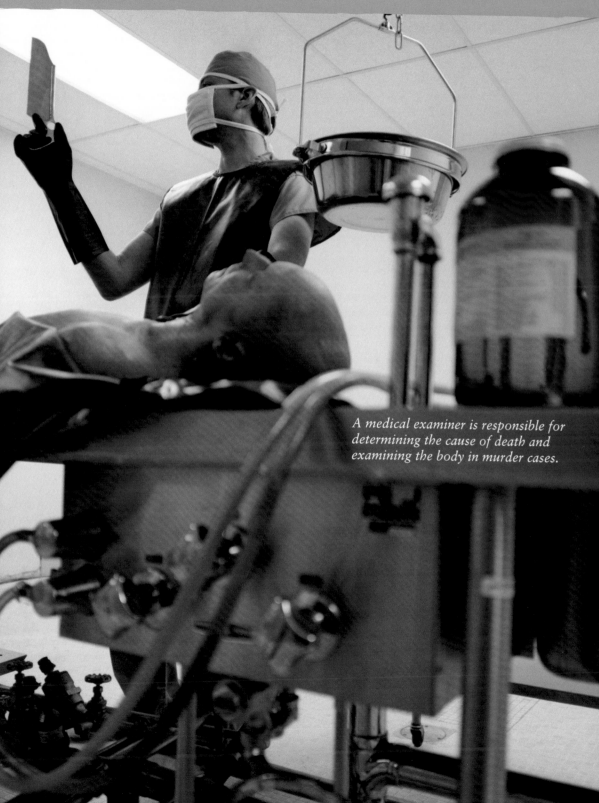

A medical examiner is responsible for determining the cause of death and examining the body in murder cases.

Science on the TV Screen

Forensic investigators and analysts who create DNA profiles are often asked how the reality of their work compares to the stylized drama of the increasingly popular genre of police procedural TV shows, such as *CSI* and *Bones*. One major difference the real CSIs cite is that in real crime investigations, the investigators who collect evidence at crime scenes generally do not interview witnesses and chase down criminals, and investigators do not analyze the samples that the CSI unit collects at the crime scene. That task is carried out by trained analysts who generally remain in the lab, analyzing and processing evidence from many sources at once.

TV dramas also show DNA analysis happening much faster and easier than it does in real life. Moreover, due to budgetary restraints, most real-life crime labs are understaffed and underfunded, resulting in large backlogs of work, which makes solving crimes an even slower process. In fact, there are currently tens of thousands, possibly hundreds of thousands, of sexual assault evidence kits—the samples taken from women who report that they have been raped—sitting untested in crime labs and at police storage facilities. Some labs are trying to fix this by hiring more workers and using new technology, such as robots that can analyze DNA faster than a human can.

be useful—hair, blood, fingerprints, and more—and bring it back to the lab to be analyzed. The medical examiner, if onsite, goes over the crime scene with a physician's eye and examines the body to determine the cause and pronounced time of death. The pronounced time of death is the time at which the person is declared dead by law enforcement or medical personnel.

Elementary, Dear Watson

Only a few trained experts knew about and understood the principles advocated by Taylor; the general public was unaware of them. That changed rather abruptly in the late 1800s, however, thanks to a talented Scottish mystery writer named Sir Arthur Conan Doyle. Between 1887 and 1927, Conan Doyle wrote several stories and books featuring the world's most famous fictional detective: Sherlock Holmes.

Conan Doyle based the character on one of his college professors, Dr. Joseph Bell, who—along with Taylor—was a pioneer of forensic science. In fact, Bell often used the word "elementary," which means simple, when describing a successful diagnosis—something Sherlock Holmes became famous for saying.

Like Taylor, Bell, and other real forensic experts of that time, Holmes paid

Sir Arthur Conan Doyle (shown here), the creator of famous fictional detective Sherlock Holmes, helped bring detective work into the public eye.

close and detailed attention to evidence at crime scenes. In Conan Doyle's *A Study in Scarlet*, for instance, Holmes's sidekick, Dr. Watson, says of Holmes: "His nimble fingers were flying here, there, and everywhere, feeling, pressing, unbuttoning, examining [everything at the crime scene]."[2] Of course, today's forensic scientists would never touch crime scene evidence with their bare hands, but at the time Conan Doyle was writing his stories, investigators were unaware of how important it was not to contaminate a crime scene with their own DNA and fingerprints.

Holmes's meticulous forensic detective work captured the public imagination and remains popular even today, as TV shows such as *Sherlock* and *Elementary* make clear. In a way, all later CSIs and other forensic scientists followed in Holmes's footsteps, combining scientific inquiry with deductive thinking. Because Conan Doyle did not know of the existence of DNA, Holmes never used DNA analysis to solve crimes. It was not until the 1950s, a little more than two decades after Conan Doyle's death, that the existence of DNA was discovered, and it was not used in crime solving until the 1980s.

DNA Evidence in Popular Culture

The use of DNA evidence in solving crimes came into the public consciousness in the 1990s as the result of a murder trial that became the center of public discussion: the Orenthal James, or O.J., Simpson trial in 1995. A former football star, Simpson was accused—and eventually found innocent—of murdering his ex-wife, Nicole Brown Simpson, and Ronald Goldman. Millions of people watched the prosecutors and defense attorneys argue the facts of the case, including DNA evidence. This trial was later dramatized in 2016 in the popular TV show *American Crime Story: The People v. O.J. Simpson.*

CSI, a TV show about forensic scientists in Las Vegas, Nevada, appeared in 2000, a few years after the O.J. Simpson trial. Its producers hoped to tap into the increasing public awareness of and interest in forensics and DNA. *CSI* was hugely successful, becoming the highest-rated show on television. It was so popular that it aired for 15 years, and 3 spin-offs were created: *CSI: Miami*, *CSI: New York*, and *CSI: Cyber*.

Today, largely as a result of these and other detective shows, public faith in the use of DNA evidence to solve crime has risen drastically. According to real CSIs, that confidence is sometimes a little misplaced. In truth, they point out, these shows sometimes glamorize forensics and exaggerate the capabilities and speed of DNA analysis and other forensic techniques. As one

CSI *was the start of a whole new genre of popular TV.*

observer put it, this gives many viewers "impossibly high expectations of how easily and conclusively criminal cases can be solved using DNA analysis and other forensic science."[3]

Nevertheless, DNA evidence can be a vital tool used by investigators to solve crimes that otherwise might not have been solved. Of equal importance is DNA evidence's ability to clear innocent people who have been mistakenly convicted of crimes. DNA evidence can allow investigators to conclusively prove someone's presence at a crime scene—or their absence. According to former Manhattan Assistant District Attorney Harlan Levy, DNA evidence "can avoid many miscarriages of justice that might occur without it, in a world where the truth is often hidden and elusive."[4]

Chapter One
The Early Days of DNA

In order to understand how investigators use DNA as evidence, it is important to understand what DNA is. Essentially, DNA is the material that makes up genes. Genes determine the characteristics of a human, plant, or animal. In humans, genes determine things such as hair color, whether a person needs glasses, what kinds of diseases a person might be at risk for, and even certain parts of someone's personality. Often, it is combinations of genes that make people who they are, and many of these are influenced by the way a person grows up. For example, a person with a particular combination of genes may be at risk for getting cancer, and a poor lifestyle may increase that risk—but there is no single cancer gene a doctor could flip on or off like a switch.

Every human's DNA is made up of four compounds, which are called adenine, guanine, thymine, and cytosine. Adenine always pairs with thymine, and guanine always pairs with cytosine. However, the order in which these pairs appear in a person's DNA is unique to everyone. Even identical twins may have small differences in their DNA. Figuring out in which order these pairs appear in a DNA molecule is called DNA sequencing, and this is how forensic scientists can tell who was at a crime scene.

Police Work Before DNA Profiling

Until the 1980s, police detectives investigating crimes were limited to collecting, examining, and interpreting a small range of evidence. They could collect and examine fingerprints, for instance—but not all criminals leave fingerprints, and it can be difficult to determine which fingerprints are related to the crime and which are not, especially if the crime occurred in a public place. Fingerprints can also easily smudge, making them unreadable, and they are far from permanent. In addition, only a small fraction of people have their fingerprints on

Occupation: Forensic DNA Analyst

Job Description:
A forensic DNA analyst works mostly in a forensics lab, where they perform DNA tests on biological material that police investigators submit to the lab. The analyst also interprets the results of the DNA tests.

Education:
DNA analysts are required to have at least an associate's degree in chemistry, biology, or forensic science, but a bachelor's degree or in some cases, a master's degree is preferred. With a bachelor's degree and two years of experience, a person can choose to take a test to become certified with the American Board of Criminalistics.

Qualifications:
In addition to a college degree, in most cases, a forensic DNA analyst must have experience doing DNA casework (for example, collecting samples), be familiar with lab equipment, and have strong verbal and written communication skills.

Additional Information:
The DNA analyst must be prepared to give expert testimony in court when called on to do so. They must also be able to periodically check the reliability of lab equipment and procedures and to help train new analysts hired by the lab.

Salary:
The average salary for a forensic DNA analyst in 2017 was $37,000 to $85,000.

record, so even when police are able to recover fingerprints from a crime scene, they sometimes have no way to make a match. This is why police will often ask suspects for their fingerprints—if they are a match to prints at the crime scene, investigators can reasonably argue that the suspect was present.

Investigators could also collect and examine blood samples from a crime scene—a technique called blood-typing. They might find some traces of type B-positive blood and some traces of type A-positive blood at a murder scene, for example. After taking a sample of the victim's blood and finding that it was B-positive, they could conclude that the A-positive blood most likely came from the murderer. However, this technique is limited in its usefulness. First, hundreds of millions of people in the world have A-positive blood, so in theory, anyone with A-positive blood living in the area

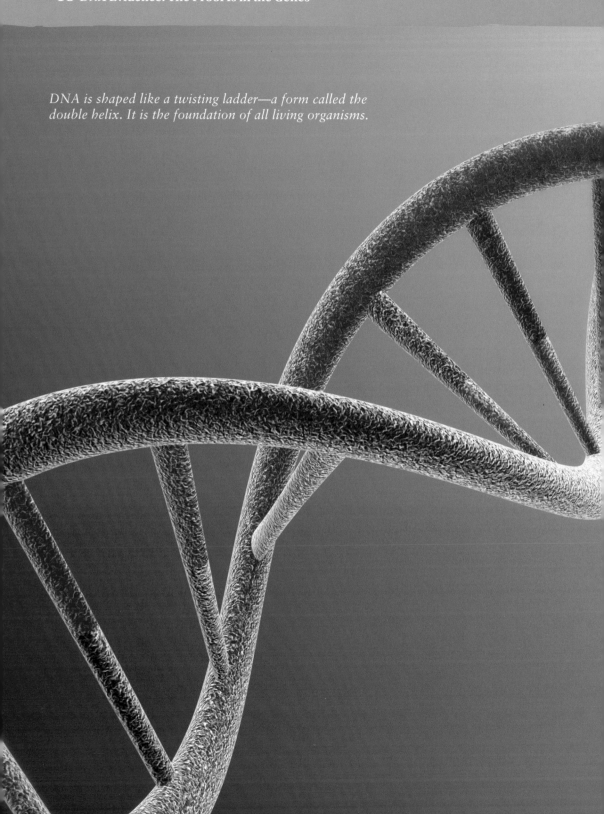

DNA is shaped like a twisting ladder—a form called the double helix. It is the foundation of all living organisms.

where the murder occurred might be the guilty party. Additionally, sometimes multiple blood samples at crime scenes get mixed together. If types A and B combine, it can often look like blood type AB, making blood-typing in that case useless.

What crime investigators needed was a forensic technique that was far more precise and conclusive than either fingerprinting or blood-typing. They needed a way to zero in on and more firmly identify a culprit from among thousands of potential suspects. This is what they got when DNA profiling was introduced in the mid-to-late 1980s. The technique is also referred to as DNA fingerprinting, genetic fingerprinting, DNA analysis, DNA forensics, and DNA testing.

Whatever one chooses to call it, the use of DNA to solve crimes has revolutionized police work and legal systems in countries around the world. This is because of the special nature of DNA, a core part of the genetic blueprints of living organisms. Because the DNA of everyone in the world is unique, one person's DNA, in theory, can be differentiated from the DNA of everyone else. This gives forensic scientists, police, lawyers, and judges a far better chance of identifying each individual present at a crime scene with a high degree of certainty and making sure these lawbreakers are punished.

Therefore, the discovery of DNA and its application to crime solving make up one of the great triumphs of modern science.

DNA Discoveries and Heredity

The development of DNA profiling began in 1952. That year, two American researchers, Alfred Hershey and Martha Chase, made an important discovery. Working in their Cold Spring Harbor Laboratory in Long Island, New York, the researchers studied a substance found in the bodies of all living things: DNA. Between 1869 and 1950, a number of researchers around the world had isolated DNA and studied it. However, no one was quite sure exactly what its purpose was. Until Hershey and Chase's breakthrough, the connection between DNA and heredity—the passing on of traits from one generation to the next—had not been proven conclusively (without a doubt).

The most popular theory at the time was that certain proteins controlled heredity. However, Hershey and Chase made a vital discovery: They proved that DNA is a genetic material carrying some of the blueprints of life. The exact manner in which DNA determines the genetic makeup of people and animals was still uncertain at this point because the structure of the DNA molecule remained a mystery.

Hoping to solve this mystery, American scientist James D. Watson and English scientist Francis Crick began intensively studying DNA. At the same time, British scientists Maurice Wilkins and Rosalind Franklin began working on a similar project. At some point between 1951 and 1953, Wilkins showed Watson X-ray photographs of DNA that Franklin had taken, along with her notes. Seeing them, Watson pieced together the solution. Watson and Crick published their findings in 1953 without crediting Franklin's work. Their article correctly proposed that the DNA of people and animals is stored in the nucleus, or center, of nearly every cell in the body. DNA molecules are bigger than other molecules and uniquely shaped. Each DNA molecule consists of two long strands of genetic material. One strand comes from a person's mother and the other from their father. In that way, every person inherits some genetic information from each parent. Franklin published her work in a supporting article in the same issue of the journal, but history gave Watson and Crick all the credit.

How Many Helixes?

The two strands inside each DNA molecule twist around each other, forming a winding spiral that scientists call a

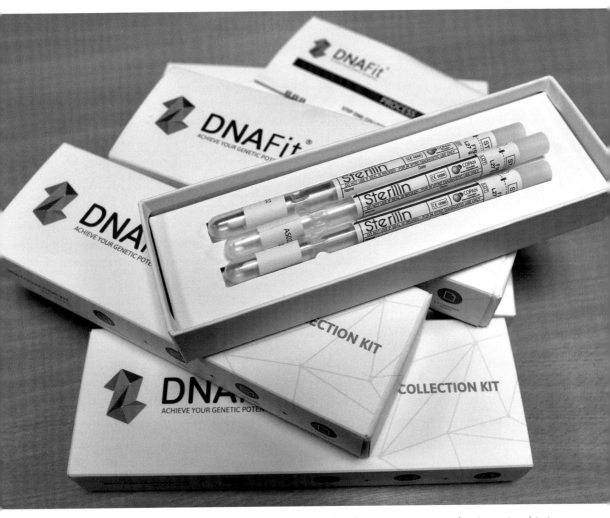

DNA testing can help determine the relationship between two people. A testing kit is shown here.

double helix. This double helix looks like a twisting ladder because the two strands are connected in thousands of places by little rungs. Each rung is composed of two parts, called nucleotide bases, and each grouping of two is called a base pair. In all, a typical DNA molecule has about 3 billion base pairs, for a total of about 6 billion bases.

These bases are always made up of the same four chemicals—guanine (G), cytosine (C), thymine (T), and adenine (A). The chemicals arrange themselves on the DNA ladder in varying patterns, called sequences, which can be short or long. One example of a short sequence is AGCTCAATCG.

The chemical sequences that extend through the base pairs of a DNA molecule form small bits of genetic information, and each of these bits determines part of the complex blueprint for constructing the body of one person or animal. These pieces or sections of DNA that contain all the information needed to make these changes are called genes. Thus, each gene consists of a series of chemical sequences that exist alongside one another on the double helix, and together they perform a single genetic task. Genes can take multiple forms, which are called alleles. Everyone inherits one allele for each gene from their mother and one from their father. For example, every human has a gene for hair color, but not everyone has the same allele. If someone's mother has brown hair while their father has blond hair, the person will inherit the brown hair allele and the blond hair allele. They cannot inherit a red hair allele unless a blood relative in their family has red hair.

Many people believe each gene has a specific task, but researchers now know this is not always true. Some traits, such as eye color, are monogenic, or controlled by just one gene. Others are polygenic—requiring multiple genes to work together. Even something as simple as whether a person is right-handed or left-handed is polygenic. Most traits are also influenced by a person's environment. According to the website Learn.Genetics,

Multiple studies present evidence that handedness is controlled by many genes—at least 30 and as many as 100—each with a small effect; many are linked to brain development. Environment also plays an important role: some cultures actively discourage left-handedness.[5]

Sometimes traits that are monogenic show up in a person as a type of disorder or disability. For example, color blindness is monogenic, and so is a very rare type of diabetes called neonatal diabetes mellitus (NDM), which is diabetes that an infant is born with. Other diseases and disorders, such as the more common type 1 and type 2 diabetes, are polygenic.

The ability to understand and distinguish individual genes and alleles is essential in DNA profiling. All the base pairs, chemical sequences, genes, and alleles in the DNA of humans add up to the genetic code—what makes each individual person who they are. The complete human genetic code is called the human genome.

By the Numbers

6.5–10 feet

(2–3 m)
length of each strand
of DNA in each cell of
a human or animal

Sir Alec Jeffreys and the 0.1 Percent

In the years following the work of Franklin, Wilkins, Watson, and Crick describing the DNA double helix, it became clear that close to 99.9 percent of the human genome is identical in all people. Therefore, only one-tenth of 1 percent of the sequences, genes, and alleles are different. When it comes to genes, people are more like everyone else in the world than they are different.

However, these small differences are what distinguish one person from another. One-tenth of 1 percent may not sound like much, but it consists of about 3 million base pairs. When these are arranged in different ways, they can produce billions or trillions of possible variations. This is how people can be so diverse despite having 99.9 percent of the same genetic sequencing.

It was this one-tenth of 1 percent and its many potential variations that attracted the interest of the father of DNA profiling, English geneticist Sir Alec Jeffreys. Jeffreys began working at a lab at the University of Leicester in 1977. In the years that followed, he and his colleagues studied genes and how they evolved and changed. This led him to look at sections of the DNA double helix that seemed to be different in different individuals, called highly variable regions. Within these areas are short chemical sequences that came to be called minisatellites.

Jeffreys searched for ways to better observe these minisatellites. "We made a probe that should latch onto lots of these minisatellites at the same time,"[6] he explained. Then, in September 1984, the researchers used an X-ray machine, like that used by dentists and doctors, to take a picture of what the probe had revealed. Jeffreys recalled,

I took one look, thought, "what a complicated mess," then suddenly realized we had patterns ... There was a level of individual specificity that was light years beyond anything that had been seen before ... Standing in front of this picture in the darkroom, my life took a complete turn.[7]

Jeffreys and his colleagues recognized that they had done more than

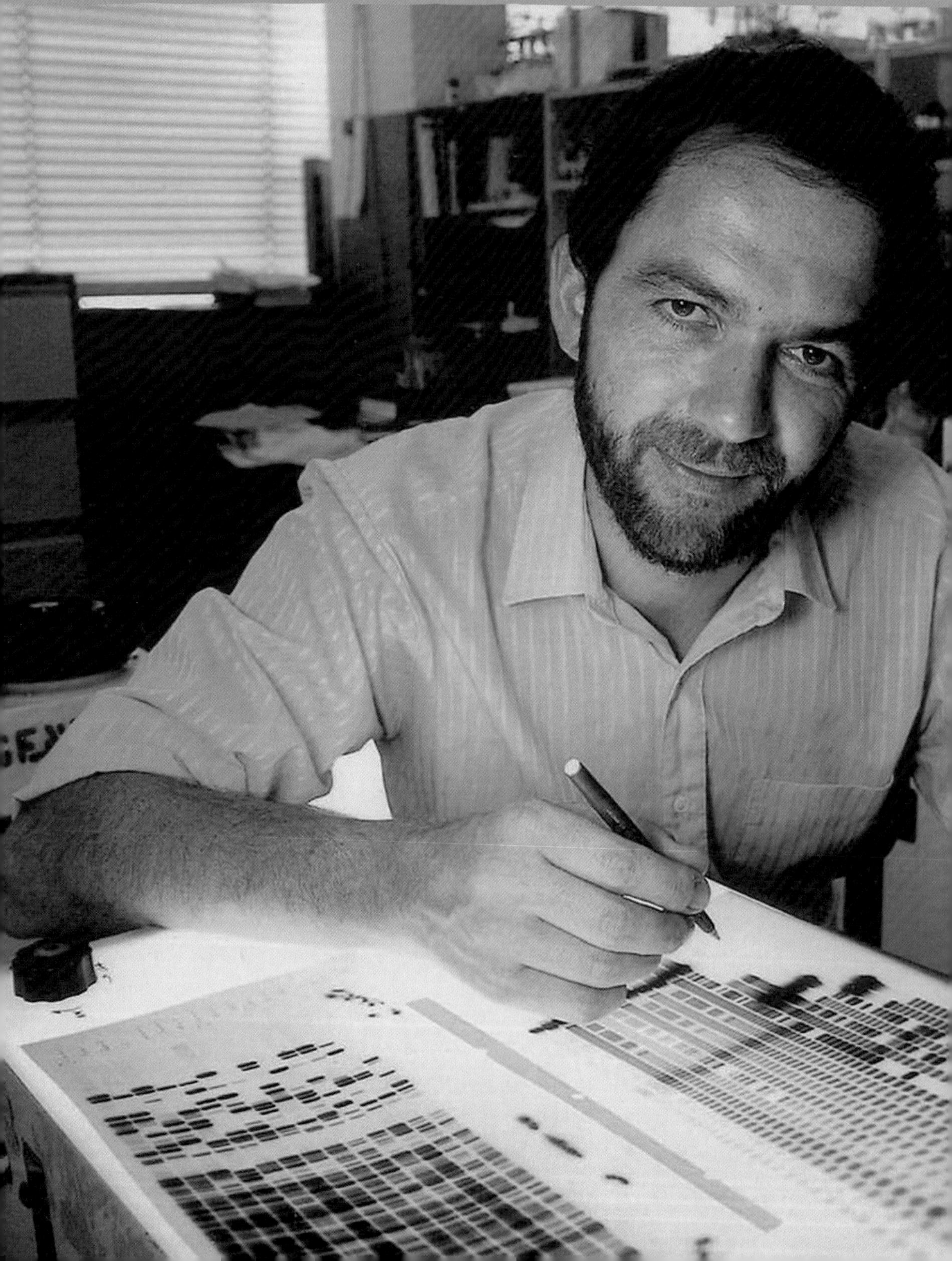

Sir Alec Jeffreys (shown here) is responsible for a major breakthrough in scientific DNA testing.

create images of areas of DNA variability, although even that was certainly a difficult and important feat that would advance the course of modern science. What Jeffreys's team had done was recognize that the patterns of minisatellites on the X-ray could be used in other areas of science, including forensic science. In particular, since these areas of DNA variability were different for each person, they could be used to distinguish one person from another. In a later interview, Jeffreys explained,

The implications for individual identification ... were obvious ... It was clear that these hypervariable DNA patterns offered the promise of a truly individual-specific identification system ... For the first time [there was] a general method for getting at large numbers of highly variable regions of human DNA. Also, almost as an accidental by-product, it suggested approaches for not only developing genetic markers for medical genetic research, but for opening up the whole field of forensic DNA typing.[8]

The DNA Detective

Alec Jeffreys, the inventor of DNA analysis, was born on January 9, 1950, in Oxford, England. As a young man, he attended the University of Oxford, and in 1977, he began working at the biological labs at the University of Leicester. It was at Leicester in 1984 that he was able to separate DNA fragments into recognizable patterns and record them using an X-ray machine. This process, called restriction fragment length polymorphism (RFLP), remained the standard method of DNA analysis for several years.

Having made significant scientific discoveries, Jeffreys was elected to a prestigious scientific organization, the Royal Society, in 1986, and in 1994, the English queen knighted him, making him Sir Alec Jeffreys. He also won the Albert Einstein World Award of Science in 1996 and the Copley Medal of the Royal Society in 2014, which is awarded for outstanding achievements in science.

Why DNA Testing Matters

By "forensic DNA typing," Jeffreys meant a way of using DNA in the same way detectives used fingerprints to seek out and arrest criminals. It makes sense, then, that he coined the term "genetic fingerprinting," which became a process now commonly called DNA profiling. This new technology seemed to possess a number of distinct and remarkable advantages for investigators trying to identify suspects in criminal cases. First, the chances of any two people having identical DNA, especially in the variable region of minisatellites, is extremely tiny. Therefore, DNA tests produce a genetic snapshot that can single out one suspect from all other suspects. Former prosecutor Harlan Levy explained the mathematical probabilities involved:

It may be that a DNA fragment [group of minisatellites] in one sample that could be expected to occur in one person in 100 ... matches a fragment in [another] sample. That is significant but hardly overwhelming. But if there is a DNA match at another location [on the DNA helix taken from the samples], the numbers suddenly grow exponentially ... The chances of the two DNA profiles matching randomly are one in 10,000 ... If there is a match at a third location ... the numbers would go to 1 million. And if there is a fourth match ... it goes to one in [many millions].[9]

Similarly, if a suspect has seven, eight, or nine matches, the chances that they are not the culprit is one in hundreds of billions or even trillions. Since there are more than 7.5 billion people on Earth, it is extremely likely that the suspect is the guilty party.

Additionally, Jeffreys and his colleagues soon realized a second advantage of DNA profiling: Nearly every cell in the human body has a nucleus that contains DNA. This means that almost any cell from a suspect, such as a skin cell, hair cell, saliva cell, or urine cell, carries the suspect's genetic fingerprint. This vastly expands the diversity of trace evidence—tiny amounts of evidence, such as a single hair—that might be found at a crime scene and analyzed, thereby increasing the likelihood of identifying the criminal. It also increases analysts' ability to match trace evidence found at the scene of the crime with the person who committed the crime. Because the same DNA can be found in every cell with a nucleus, analysts can take a sample of saliva from a suspect to match with skin or hair cells found at the crime scene; they do not have to take samples from the same part of the body to get a match. "Fingerprints come only from fingers," researcher Ngaire E. Genge wrote:

> But DNA can be found in blood, in urine, in feces, in saliva, in some hair, in the shed skin cells found in a facecloth or toothbrush—even in the sweatband of a hat! A suspect doesn't have to bleed at the [crime] scene to leave DNA. Semen at rape scenes, saliva on the envelope of a ransom note, skin cells scraped onto a rope while tying a victim— all provide the opportunity for collection and analysis.[10]

A third advantage of DNA collection and analysis is that DNA can survive much longer than most other kinds of evidence. Most fingerprints smudge or disappear after a few weeks or months (although on occasion they can last a few years). In comparison, DNA can, under the right circumstances, last for centuries—or even for millennia. Successful DNA analysis has been performed on Egyptian mummies up to 4,000 years old, and similar tests have been conducted on 25,000-year-old human remains found in a cave in southern Italy.

The remarkable longevity of DNA evidence allows investigators to go back and look at cold cases. These are criminal cases from 5, 10, 20, or even 50 years ago that were never solved, often due to lack of compelling evidence. If any evidence found at the crime scene is still in storage, it can be tested, and this could potentially solve the case. The culprit might be caught and jailed. If this is not possible, at least the victim's family can achieve some kind of closure.

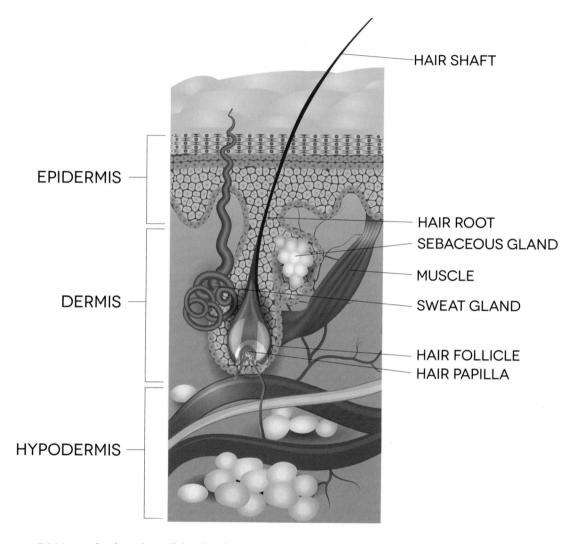

EPIDERMIS

DERMIS

HYPODERMIS

HAIR SHAFT

HAIR ROOT
SEBACEOUS GLAND
MUSCLE
SWEAT GLAND

HAIR FOLLICLE
HAIR PAPILLA

DNA can be found in all kinds of places, including hair follicles (although it cannot be found in hair shafts).

Yet another advantage of DNA is its ability to indicate familial, or family, relationships. Because each person inherits some DNA from each parent, their DNA is very similar to, though not exactly the same as, their parents'. A person's DNA is also similar to their siblings' DNA, and, to a lesser degree, to any aunts, uncles, and cousins.

A murder case that occurred in the Philippines illustrated how this can be helpful to crime investigators. Two people committed the murder, but only one was identified by an eyewitness and arrested. Some saliva found at the crime scene was analyzed, and the DNA it contained was very similar, but not an exact match, to the DNA of the man in custody; this showed that the second killer was almost certainly one of this man's close relatives. Based on this, police questioned the man's brother, who soon confessed to his role in the crime.

By the Numbers

19,000

number of genes in the human genome

Unleashing DNA's Potential

The case of the two brothers was not the first to use DNA samples to solve a murder. That distinction went to two related cases that occurred in England in the 1980s, which Jeffreys was instrumental in solving. The first murder took place in November 1983. A 15-year-old schoolgirl named Lynda Mann went missing in the village of Narborough, only 6 miles (9.7 km) from Jeffreys's lab. The next morning, someone found the girl's body on a footpath in the local woods. The coroner—an official who examines

dead bodies—determined that she had been strangled to death. There were also semen stains on her body, indicating that a rape had occurred. Unfortunately, no other evidence was found—no fingerprints, clothing fibers, or forgotten items. The semen was all the police had to go on. However, because DNA profiling did not yet exist, there was no way to tell whose semen it was, so the case could not be solved.

The situation changed when, three years later in July 1986, 15-year-old Dawn Ashworth was murdered in the same village. Two days after she was reported missing, police found her body. Like Mann, she had been strangled and raped. Police arrested Richard Buckland, who worked at a nearby hospital. Witnesses had seen a man matching his description near the scene of the murder a few days before, and Buckland had knowledge of unreleased details about Ashworth's murder.

Under intense questioning, he finally confessed that he had raped and strangled Ashworth. Due to similarities in the methods and details of the Ashworth and Mann murders, the police suspected that Buckland had committed both crimes. However, Buckland continued to deny that he had committed the earlier crime.

One of the detectives remembered reading about the recent discovery of DNA analysis. Hoping for a break in the case, the police delivered a sample of the semen found on Mann and a sample of Buckland's blood to Jeffreys, who analyzed the DNA in both samples. The DNA of Mann's killer did not match Buckland's DNA, so Buckland could not be the murderer in that case—but even more surprising were the results when Jeffreys analyzed the semen found on Ashworth and compared it to Buckland's DNA: There was no match. This meant Buckland had not killed either girl and had falsely confessed to the second murder. The police saw no other choice but to release him from custody. "I have no doubt whatsoever," Jeffreys later said, "that he would have been found guilty had it not been for DNA evidence. That was a remarkable occurrence."[11]

The police were disappointed. Rather than solving two crimes with one killer, they suddenly had no suspects for either

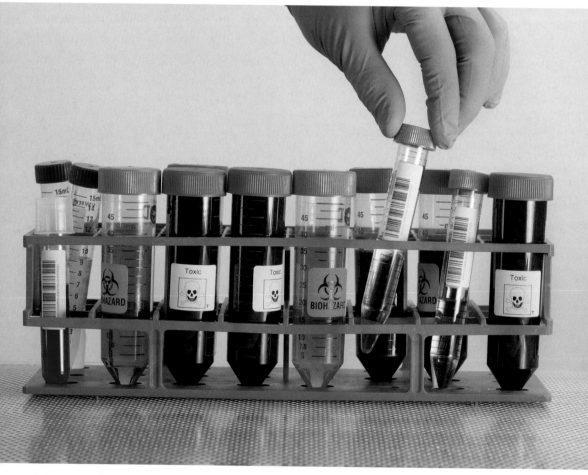

DNA samples collected at crime scenes are brought to labs, where they are analyzed.

murder and had to start from scratch on both cases. However, this time, they were armed with the new DNA technology. Early in 1987, they began testing blood and semen samples from every man they could find in Narborough and surrounding villages. They did not find a match until they learned that a local bakery worker, Colin Pitchfork, had paid another man to submit his own blood and claim it was Pitchfork's.

The police arrested Pitchfork in September, and he confessed to both murders. Jeffreys then administered new DNA tests to confirm the confession, and the tests showed that Pitchfork's DNA exactly matched the DNA in the semen found on both dead girls. According to Harlan Levy,

> It was an extraordinarily auspicious [promising] beginning for the new technology. In its first known application in a murder case, DNA testing fulfilled both its promises, clearing an innocent man and helping convict a guilty one ... DNA testing was completely new, but there was no doubt about its potential within the criminal justice system. Prosecutors and the press rushed to embrace the novel tool.[12]

Today, that tool is a standard and vital one used by law enforcement officials across the United States and in many other nations.

By the Numbers

10

number of genes that separate mice and humans

Chapter Two
How to Build a DNA Profile

The process of DNA profiling involves a number of steps that must be taken in a specific order. Some of them are complex, and all of them require considerable skill and deliberate care. CSIs and other experts who work with DNA samples must be highly educated and specially trained. These investigators and lab technicians generally have college degrees in biology, chemistry, genetics, forensic science, or some related scientific field. Moreover, some crime labs will only hire a DNA specialist who has a minimum of six months to one year of on-the-job experience. This experience can be learned in a noncriminal setting; for example, some hospitals hire DNA analysts to test for genetic diseases.

All this training is necessary because it is vital that samples are handled with extreme care during every step of the profiling process. It is very easy to contaminate a sample. A DNA sample that has been contaminated or mishandled cannot be used as evidence in a court of law. If the sample was one that was taken from the crime scene, there is no way to get another one, and the suspect may be set free even if they are guilty. In the same way, contamination of a DNA sample might result in someone who was mistakenly sent to jail losing their only chance to be freed.

The steps in the DNA profiling process used by these dedicated specialists can be grouped into two general categories: collecting evidence at a crime scene and analyzing the samples back at the lab. When collecting samples, investigators follow strict guidelines designed to ensure that nothing is missed and that all evidence is properly handled. At the lab, technicians follow a standardized procedure to ensure that results are permissible in court.

Where Can DNA Be Found?

At a crime scene, police often use bright yellow tape to mark the area that needs to be inspected by officials and to protect it from passers-by. The fewer people who interact with the crime scene before investigators arrive, the better; in this way, police can ensure that any evidence collected will be relevant to the case and will remain uncontaminated.

The most common sources of DNA evidence are blood, semen, saliva, and skin. Skin cells can be found in multiple ways, including if the culprit has dandruff or was injured while committing the crime. Red blood cells have no nuclei and therefore do not contain DNA; however, white blood cells do contain DNA, so when CSIs collect blood samples, they analyze the white blood cells to build a DNA profile. The same is true of hair. Although hairs are often found at crime scenes, the cells in the shaft, or main part of the hair, have no DNA. However, if a hair has been pulled out by the root—which can happen if the victim fights back against their attacker— DNA can be found in the skin cells on the root.

Bones, teeth, urine, and feces also contain DNA. These are less commonly found at crime scenes, but they can help investigators in other ways. For example, dental records and DNA taken from the victim's teeth can help investigators identify a body.

To find these vehicles for DNA, investigators begin looking in a number of obvious places at a crime scene. Saliva, for example, is often found on items that typically interact with the mouth, such as the rims of cups and glasses, silverware, toothbrushes, telephone receivers, and cigarette butts. The most common places investigators find semen specimens are the genital areas of rape victims, bed sheets, and discarded condoms. Likewise, skin cells or blood from violent criminals are frequently found under the fingernails of victims who scratched them while resisting. Traces of incriminating blood are often discovered in the cracks between floorboards after a criminal has tried to clean up a crime scene.

DNA evidence can also turn up in places that are far less obvious and at times even surprising to untrained observers. For instance, valuable biological evidence can sometimes be found in the bathroom trash. A wastebasket can contain discarded tissues, cotton swabs, and other items containing traces of bodily cells or fluids. Similarly, contact lenses are typically coated with fluid from the wearer's eyes, and envelopes that someone licked might still contain

DNA can be found in many places; one of the most common is on the rims of recently used cups or mugs.

traces of that person's saliva.

It might seem logical that urine samples would most likely be found in the bathroom, especially in, on, or around the toilet. Although this is often the case, experienced CSIs know they should also look elsewhere—especially when the crime scene is in a natural setting. According to one veteran investigator who collected DNA at crime scenes for 18 years,

After working a bunch of crimes that took us to cabins and other woodsy locations, we eventually came to the conclusion that, if you put ten guys in the woods and they've got to [urinate], nine of those ten guys will prefer to pee on a tree trunk ... shine a source light around a campsite and I'll guarantee you there'll be DNA from urine on some tree somewhere [in the area].[13]

Gathering the Evidence

When CSIs first arrive at a crime scene, they do not know which items and materials are going to

Hair, Kitty Kitty

DNA makes up the genetic material of all animals, not just humans, which can occasionally help forensic scientists solve crimes by ruling out or convicting a human suspect. Forensic science researcher Ngaire E. Genge wrote about a case in which cat hair allowed police to convict a murderer:

One of the first cases linking two people through non-human DNA was investigated by the Royal Canadian Mounted Police (RCMP). While investigating a death in Prince Edward Island, examiners recovered two white hairs, which were at first thought to be those of the victim's ex-husband. They weren't. They were cat hairs. Not having a unit that dealt with cat DNA, the RCMP sent the hairs, as well as a blood sample from the ex-husband's white cat, to the National Cancer Institute's Cat Genome Project in Maryland. The lab there confirmed that both blood and fur came from the same cat, and the ex-husband was convicted of murder.[1]

1. Ngaire E. Genge, *The Forensic Casebook: The Science of Crime Scene Investigation.* New York, NY: Ballantine, 2002, p. 150.

produce DNA evidence that will solve the crime. They might find a used napkin or some stray hairs, for example, but the presence of someone's DNA does not automatically make them a criminal. It might turn out that these belonged to the victim or an innocent bystander, not the suspect.

For this reason, the guidelines for evidence collection require that a wide range of items and biological materials be collected at the crime scene. These can be sorted through and analyzed later at the lab to determine whether or not they are important to the case. The U.S. National Institute of Justice (a division of the U.S. Department of Justice in Washington, D.C.) issues a checklist of DNA-related items and materials that investigators should look for at a crime scene. The list includes fingernails, paper towels, tissues, Q-tips, toothpicks, straws, cigarette butts, blankets, sheets, mattresses, pillows, dirty laundry, eyeglasses, contact lenses, cell phones, ropes, stamped envelopes, used condoms, and more.

According to the collection guidelines, investigators must make sure they do not touch any of the evidence with their bare hands or fingers in order to prevent an investigator's own cells and fluids from contaminating the evidence. The person doing the collecting should wear rubber gloves and change them often. For the same reason, investigators should be careful not to touch their face, hair, glasses, and so forth while wearing the gloves. All of these often thoughtless gestures can result in contamination of a DNA sample—for example, if an investigator touches their mouth and some of their saliva transfers onto the gloves they are using to collect samples, they may have made that sample unusable.

In addition to gloves, investigators are expected to use clean disposable items, such as cotton swabs, small wooden sticks, or wooden tweezers to pick up the evidence. For instance, an investigator will not use the same swab to collect two different samples; that way, one piece of evidence does not contaminate another.

Once they have picked up the evidence, the investigator places it in a clean paper evidence bag. This paper bag is important because airtight containers or plastic bags can create moisture in the container that can compromise the evidence. In addition, the evidence must be allowed time to dry before being sealed in a paper bag so it does not decompose. The bag must be clearly labeled, indicating both what the evidence is and where it was found.

That helps eliminate mistakes later in the lab, such as accidentally mixing up two or more samples. A biohazard symbol and label must also be placed on the bag to warn people at a glance that it contains potentially dangerous material. For instance, diseases can be transmitted through a person's blood or saliva, so care must be taken when handling this evidence.

Guidelines recommend that while handling and packaging evidence, investigators should try as hard as they can not to sneeze, cough, or even talk. All of these activities spray tiny saliva droplets. Though they are nearly invisible to the human eye, they can land on and contaminate the evidence. For this reason, many investigators wear surgical masks while handling evidence at a crime scene.

Evidence is not the only thing that must be protected at crime scenes. The investigators and lab technicians must also be careful when handling evidence that might cause them harm. CSIs, Genge pointed out, regularly handle a number of bodily fluids that could be carrying disease, germs, and other harmful biohazards: "Biohazards like hepatitis and HIV are real dangers to investigators and laboratory personnel who handle bio-wastes and bio-fluids, so all samples must be treated as infectious until proven otherwise."[14]

Crime scene investigators label everything and cover themselves up as much as possible to avoid their own DNA getting mixed in with samples from the crime scene.

EVIDENCE BAG

Back at the Lab

All evidence samples found and collected at a crime scene are sent immediately to the nearest forensics lab. Once there, the first step is for technicians to go through each sample to make sure all the evidence is biological material that has the potential to contain DNA. Quite often, it is easy to identify where a sample might have come from; for example, a pool of dark red liquid lying beside a bullet hole or gash in a dead person's head is almost certainly going to be blood. It is also generally safe to assume that yellow stains found on the rim of a toilet seat are urine.

However, investigators cannot always be sure what a substance really is until it is tested in the lab. In rare cases, for instance, a yellow stain on a toilet could be residue of a non-biological liquid that someone spilled there. Similarly, hairs found at a crime scene might have neither human nor animal origins; instead, they might be synthetic (man-made) fibers from a wig. To avoid wrongly categorizing substances such as these, lab technicians run a brief preliminary test to identify it. This can save both time and money. As forensic DNA experts Norah Rudin and Keith Inman wrote, "It would be wasteful to run a full spectrum of DNA tests only to find no result because ketchup or shoe polish was analyzed."[15]

Once all the evidence samples are satisfactorily identified, it is time to test the relevant ones for DNA. To do this, the DNA must be extracted, or separated from, the cells of the blood, semen, hair roots, bone marrow, or other biological material involved. The extraction process is fairly simple and, depending on the method used, can take anywhere from five minutes to two hours. The fastest method is not always the best; sometimes, to get the best quality DNA sample, a more time-consuming method needs to be used. For example, if a hair follicle has dirt on it, this may lower the quality of the results of a particular method. Regardless of the method used, the process follows certain steps:

1. The cells must be separated from each other and then broken open so the DNA can be exposed.
2. The DNA must be separated from the other material in the cell.
3. Alcohol is added to the DNA to make it visible, so scientists can work with it more easily.
4. The DNA is purified (cleaned) and suspended in a solution to keep it from disintegrating.
5. The DNA is tested to determine its concentration and purity. The more concentrated and pure the sample is, the better results researchers will be able to get from future tests.

Extract DNA at Home

DNA is in every living thing—not just humans, but plants, animals, and insects as well. The website Learn.Genetics gives a simple experiment anyone can do at home to extract DNA:

- Pour ½ cup (100 mL) split peas, 1/8 teaspoon (1 mL) table salt, and 1 cup (200 mL) cold water in a blender. Blend on high for 15 seconds to separate the pea cells.
- Pour the liquid through a strainer into another container, such as a bowl or cup. Add 2 tablespoons (30 mL) of liquid detergent and swirl to mix. Let sit for 5 to 10 minutes, then pour into test tubes or other glass containers, such as toothpick holders. Fill each container one-third full.
- Add a very small amount of meat tenderizer, pineapple juice, or contact lens cleaning solution to each container, and stir gently. These substances are enzymes that will isolate the DNA.
- Tilt the container and slowly pour rubbing alcohol down the side until the container is equally full of alcohol and the pea mixture. Where the alcohol and water layers meet, there should be clumps of a white, stringy substance. These are DNA molecules, and they can be collected with a toothpick or straw and saved in a container of rubbing alcohol.

Having extracted the DNA, the technician divides it into separate samples. Most of these will be used for analysis. Generally one sample is stored in a freezer; that way, the lab can study it months or years later if, for legal or technical reasons, the criminal investigation requires it.

DNA Analysis

There are multiple valid methods of analyzing extracted DNA samples; more likely than not, this process will continue to evolve and improve as DNA becomes more ingrained in the investigative process. The oldest method of analysis, introduced by Jeffreys in the 1980s and still occasionally used, is restriction fragment length polymorphism (RFLP). A chemical substance called an enzyme is used to cut the long DNA strands into a number of shorter pieces, or fragments. According to Dr. Kristine Wadosky, "RFLP ... refers to the differences in DNA between people that results in us having different fragment lengths when we cut with an enzyme."[16] During the cutting process, the DNA fragments become mixed together in a disorganized jumble and are impossible to decipher. To

DNA and mtDNA

When people mention DNA and DNA analysis, they are typically talking about the principal source of DNA in the body, which is found in the nuclei of cells. However, a second form of DNA also exists, located in other parts of each cell. Called mitochondrial DNA (mtDNA), it is passed only from mother to child. For that reason, mtDNA does not change from generation to generation.

DNA analysis using mtDNA is performed fairly infrequently in most forensics labs. First, mtDNA analysis is far more expensive and time-consuming than testing that uses nuclear DNA. Also, by itself, mtDNA is not often useful in creating unique genetic profiles, mainly because nearly everyone in a given family has identical mtDNA. This means investigators cannot use it to pinpoint the exact person it came from. However, mtDNA can be useful for ruling out certain suspects or identifying bodies of known missing persons. For instance, in 2017, bones were found in Aruba that investigators believed might be the remains of Natalee Holloway, who went missing in 2005. Natalee's mother Beth gave a sample of her own DNA so investigators could test the bones to see if the mtDNA matched. If it did, they would know it was Natalee because none of the other Holloway children are missing. However, the results showed that the bones were not a match. Not only does this not solve the Holloway mystery, it raises the question of whose bones were found.

impose some order on the fragments, the technicians place them in a special gel and run an electrical current through the gel. The current causes the fragments to move, and the distance they move within the gel depends on their weight. The smaller fragments move the farthest, a process that separates them from the larger fragments. Eventually the separated fragments form distinct band-like patterns. When X-rayed, "these bands become visible," Genge explained:

It's usually these films that are seen in court. If [the fragments in] two samples come from the same person, they'll break along the same lines and come to rest in the same places. That makes a match. If they aren't in the same place, there's no match. If there are considerable similarities but no match, it's possible the samples are from related individuals.[17]

RFLP analysis has been proven to be mostly accurate and reliable. However, it does have some disadvantages. First, it is slow, requiring at least a few weeks to produce satisfactory results, which can be frustrating to police trying to

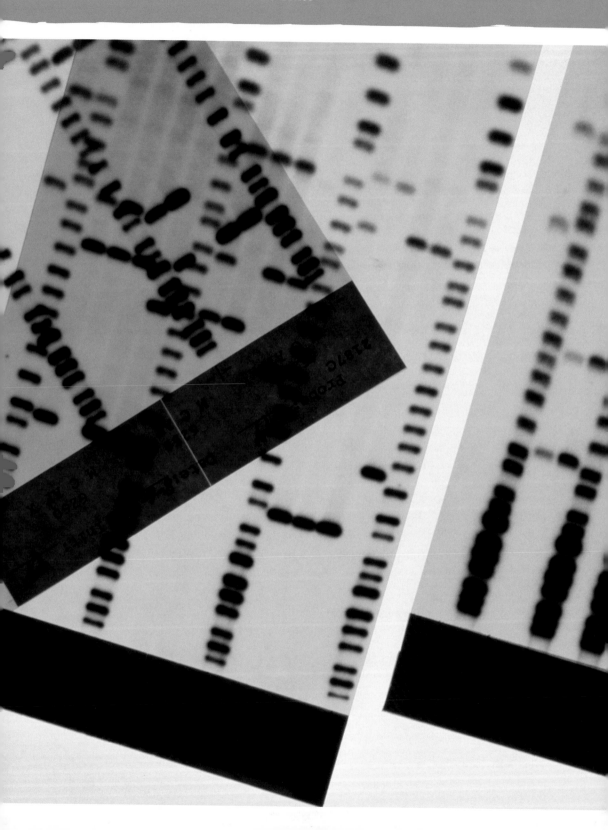

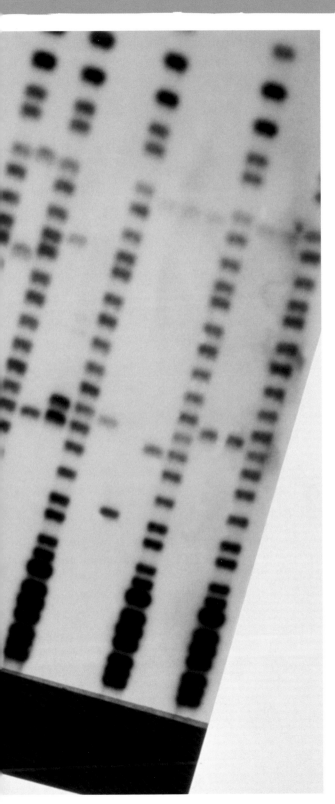

RFLP is used to create DNA sequences such as the ones shown here. Though they might look meaningless, these bands are unique to each individual.

crack a case quickly. RFLP also requires large samples of DNA, so sometimes there is not enough DNA found at the crime scene to complete the analysis. In other situations, all the DNA found must be used to complete the test, leaving none for storage.

Alternatives to RFLP

To overcome the shortcomings of RFLP analysis, scientists searched for ways both to increase the amount of DNA retrieved from samples and decrease the amount of time needed for analysis. A huge breakthrough occurred in the late 1980s when American biochemist Kary B. Mullis invented a new technique called polymerase chain reaction (PCR), for which he was awarded the Nobel Prize in chemistry in 1993. With the advent of PCR, forensic experts gained the ability to transform a tiny amount of DNA into a much larger, more workable sample.

PCR, sometimes referred to as DNA amplification, increases the amount of DNA in a sample by replicating it on the chemical level. To do this, a technician places a

Analysts sometimes use a process called PCR to analyze DNA samples.

Finding the Pattern

There are six basic steps to the DNA analysis process. They are:

1. At a crime scene, an investigator collects what might be biological evidence, including such items as hairs, blood, skin cells, saliva, and more.

2. At the lab, a technician first determines that the samples are indeed biological. Then, they extract DNA from the samples using various chemicals.

3. If the technician finds that the amount of DNA is too small to analyze properly, they use PCR to create extra DNA identical to that in the sample. During PCR, fluorescent dyes are often mixed into the sample to make the DNA stand out from the liquid in which it is suspended.

4. The DNA is placed in a specialized gel, and in a procedure called gel electrophoresis, an electrical current is passed through the gel. This separates the DNA into fragments of varying length, with the shorter fragments appearing in the bottom part of the gel.

5. The technician uses a laser beam to scan a snapshot of the gel into a computer.

6. The computer recognizes and analyzes the repeated sequences of base pairs in the DNA and produces a visual image of its unique profile. That profile can now be compared to that of a suspect or to many profiles collected in a DNA database.

small number of DNA fragments in a container and adds a special enzyme known as DNA polymerase. Using the A, C, G, and T bases in the DNA, the enzyme stimulates the DNA fragments to reproduce themselves during a process of rapid temperature changes. When the amount of DNA in the sample has doubled, the process can be repeated, producing four times as much DNA as there was in the initial sample. In this manner, the technician can create as much DNA as they want.

PCR has several benefits, the first of which is that it works very fast. A batch of DNA can be duplicated in only two or three minutes. Within two to three hours, a technician can increase the concentration of the initial sample by 50 times or more. This kind of fast work makes PCR relatively inexpensive to perform. Additionally, it can successfully replicate very small samples of DNA that, due to exposure to the

170

ATCTCTTGGCTCCAGCAT
TCATTTAGAGGAAGTAA
GAACTGTCAAAACTTT
TGTTGCTTCGGCGGCGCC
GGCCTGCCGTGGCAGATC
TCTCTTGGCTCCAGCATC
CAGCATCGATGAAGAACG
CGATACTTCTGAGTGTTC
CGGATCTCTTGGCTCCAG
ACAACGGATCTCTTGGCT
CGGATCTCTTGGCTCCAG
GATGAAGAACGCAGCGAA

STR uses repeating sequences to determine DNA profiles.

```
 '  '  '  '  |  '  '  '  '  |
0                          19
ATGAAGAACG
TCGTAACAAG
AACGGATCTC
CAAGGGTGCC
CAACGCCGGG
TGAAGAACGC
GCGAAACGCG
AGCGAACTGT
TCGATGAAGA
AGCATCGATG
TCGATGAAGA
GCGATATGTA
```

elements, have degraded in quality over many years.

Another major breakthrough occurred in the mid-1990s, with the introduction of a new method of DNA analysis: short tandem repeats, or STR. This process works by zeroing in on those sections of a DNA sample in which short sequences of base pairs repeat several times. For instance, in one person's DNA, there may be places where the sequence AATG repeats six times. In another person, this sequence may repeat only four times. By examining these areas of repetition, scientists can easily determine that the DNA of the first person is different from the second person's DNA. Used together with PCR, STR has quickly become the most often performed DNA profiling method in most forensics labs.

One significant advantage of STR analysis is that it works fairly quickly, especially when compared to RFLP analysis. Using STR, an experienced lab technician can create a DNA profile in about five or six hours. Another advantage of STR is that the short chemical sequences it uses are very stable. In fact, when exposed to the elements and other adverse conditions, these sequences can remain stable longer than entire DNA molecules can. Therefore,

STR often allows CSIs to produce DNA profiles for badly decayed bodies in which most DNA molecules have partially deteriorated.

By the Numbers

13,002,732

number of offender DNA profiles contained in the CODIS database as of 2017

A Record of DNA Profiles

Both PCR and STR have become increasingly reliable and standardized in recent years. One reason for this is the availability of commercial kits designed for use by forensic professionals. Each kit contains all the chemicals and other items needed to conduct the PCR or STR processes. Such kits have become a valuable tool in DNA profiling and its use in the conviction of criminals.

Another important tool that DNA labs use to solve crimes is a series of computerized databases. These are

Once an analyst has put together a DNA profile, they can enter it into a federal database called CODIS to see if it matches one already there.

electronic collections of DNA profile information that can easily be called up and viewed on a monitor. Each forensics lab keeps careful records of its DNA profiles and submits them to databases containing thousands of such profiles from many labs.

Individual states in America also have such databases. In addition, a federal (national) database—the Combined DNA Index System, called CODIS for short—combines information from the state databases. CODIS began as a trial program in 1990 and became fully operational in 1998. The benefit of CODIS is that DNA profiles of criminals from across the country are all stored in one place. A forensics lab in any town in the nation can tap into the system at any time. If the technicians at a lab have developed a DNA profile but cannot find a suspect to match it, they can enter that profile into CODIS. The system then compares the profile to those already compiled. The profile of a person who earlier committed a crime in another state might be a perfect match for the lab's current profile. If so, the police have a real suspect to track down. According to CODIS's official website,

Matches made among profiles in the Forensic Index can link crime scenes together, possibly identifying serial offenders. Based upon a match, police from multiple jurisdictions can coordinate their respective investigations and share the leads they developed independently.[18]

As of September 2017, CODIS contains more than 13 million DNA profiles and has assisted in more than 374,000 criminal investigations.

The ability of CODIS and other computer databases to sort through DNA profiles and solve crimes has been proven repeatedly. One of the most dramatic cases occurred in 1993, when a young woman in Cincinnati, Ohio, was raped by a man who broke into her apartment and held her at knifepoint. Investigators discovered biological evidence at the crime scene and were able to put together a DNA profile of the attacker. However, the Cincinnati police were unable to find any suspects who matched the profile.

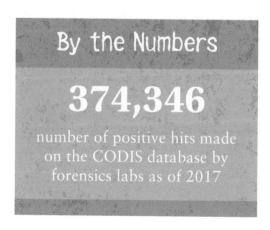

By the Numbers

374,346

number of positive hits made on the CODIS database by forensics labs as of 2017

Years passed without a break in the case. Then, in 1997, Ohio forensic scientists used CODIS to compare DNA profiles of some inmates in the state's prisons to profiles in unsolved cases. The new database quickly found a match. The profile of an inmate then serving time for burglary was identical to the profile the Cincinnati forensics lab had produced in the 1993 rape case. The inmate, Rodney J. Crooks, was about to be paroled (released early for good behavior) after serving time in jail for the burglary charge, but his parole was denied after it became clear that he had raped the woman in 1993. This and other cases like it demonstrate how modern forensics labs increasingly use rapidly advancing technology to track criminal activity across jurisdictional and even geographical lines.

Chapter Three
A Brief History of DNA Profiling

DNA profiling has been and continues to be used in a wide variety of crime-related situations and cases. Its use in investigations can be thought of in two broad categories: proving that someone committed a crime or proving that someone did not. The use of DNA evidence to clear the name of someone who has been wrongly imprisoned is as important as convicting the correct criminal in the first place. As technology continues to improve and DNA is routinely used in investigations, the criminal justice system aims to cut down on the number of false imprisonments.

This process of proving someone was falsely imprisoned is called exoneration. The first exoneration due to DNA testing in the United States occurred in 1989, and there have been 450 as of September 2017. In fact, in 1998, DNA testing was used on death row inmates in Illinois, and the results found that 13 out of 25 prisoners could be proven innocent. Then-governor George Ryan

immediately halted executions, and a study was conducted to determine how law enforcement could avoid false convictions going forward; use of DNA evidence was at the core of the study's findings. Moreover, in a few criminal cases, DNA has simultaneously convicted a guilty party and exonerated an innocent one. In the celebrated first use of DNA evidence to solve a crime, for example, Colin Pitchfork was convicted of the rape and murder of two teenage girls, and Richard Buckland was cleared as a suspect in the same crimes.

Some convictions and exonerations brought about by DNA evidence have been fairly straightforward and clearcut. Others have been more complex, with surprising twists and turns.

DNA Comes to America
The case involving Buckland and Pitchfork, which took place in England in the 1980s, sent shock waves through criminal justice systems around the

globe. Police departments far and wide were eager to learn how to use the exciting new DNA profiling technology to aid their investigations.

The first case in the United States that used DNA profiling was for Tommie Lee Andrews. In Orlando, Florida, in 1987, Andrews was arrested for breaking into a woman's home and raping her at knifepoint. DNA found at the scene, as well as at the scene of 20 other rape cases, matched DNA taken from Andrews.

The Andrews case and other early, similar cases involving DNA evidence gave American police and prosecutors a powerful new tool to use in solving cases. Forensics labs across the country quickly equipped themselves with the new technology. As a result, as time went on, the process became standard in crime scene analysis. However, lack of funding has hindered the use of DNA technology to crack down on certain types of crime, such as sexual assault. In many cases, people who report a sexual assault have DNA samples taken in the hospital, but these rape kits are sent to storage and never fully analyzed. Many states are taking steps to address the backlog and in the process, are discovering that many of the kits have the same DNA in them—that is, the same person committed multiple sexual assaults, sometimes in different states.

Before the advent of DNA profiling, police might have identified a suspect for a murder, but if that suspect denied committing the crime and the existing evidence was not strong enough to convince a jury that the suspect was guilty beyond the shadow of a doubt, nothing could be done. Such was the case of 16-year-old Sarah Johnson, daughter of Alan and Diane Johnson, residents of Bellevue, Idaho. On September 2, 2003, the elder Johnsons were shot to death in their home. Some of the detectives working on the case found out the deceased couple did not like Sarah's boyfriend, an undocumented Mexican immigrant. It seemed possible that the Johnsons were planning to turn in the young man to immigration authorities, and that might have been a motive for Sarah to kill her parents. However, though she admitted to being home at the time of the murders, she claimed she had nothing to do with them.

Sarah's claims of innocence were shown to be lies during the trial when the prosecutors introduced some incriminating DNA evidence. Police had found various blood-covered items, including a rubber glove, in a family trash barrel. Testifying on the witness stand, Cynthia Hall, a DNA analyst with the Idaho State Police, said, "The DNA profile obtained from the latex glove matched the profile obtained from the blood sample said to belong to Sarah Johnson."[19]

Sarah Johnson was found guilty in 2005 and ordered to serve two life

O.J. Simpson (shown here) was famously found innocent of murder even though his DNA matched samples taken from the crime scene.

sentences plus fifteen years without possibility of parole. In 2014, the Idaho Innocence Project—a group that works to exonerate people it believes were wrongfully accused of crimes—asked the Idaho supreme court to have another trial for Sarah. The group said new evidence and updates to DNA testing technology might prove Sarah's innocence. However, the supreme court denied the appeal; it would only have been approved if the group could have shown evidence that Sarah's lawyer made mistakes that caused her to be found guilty.

However, using DNA evidence in a criminal case does not always ensure that the person charged with the crime will be convicted. A famous example was the O.J. Simpson case in 1995. The former football star was charged with killing his former wife, Nicole Brown Simpson, and Ronald Goldman. The prosecution presented DNA evidence taken from blood samples found on a sock and glove. The prosecutors said the DNA evidence showed that the odds that Simpson was innocent were 1 in 170 million. Nevertheless, the jury found Simpson innocent. First, the jurors felt that the defense had successfully raised certain doubts about the defendant's guilt (including the fact that the bloodied glove did not seem to fit Simpson's hand). Later, several jurors admitted that they did not fully understand the meaning of the DNA evidence.

Problems with DNA Testing

Many people do not have firsthand knowledge of DNA testing, so they believe it is a foolproof way to identify a criminal. TV shows, movies, and other types of media help reinforce this belief. However, DNA testing is not 100 percent accurate, and this misplaced confidence in the technology can have dangerous consequences. According to *Popular Science*,

> *DNA evidence can be unequivocal under ideal conditions: when officials have a large quantity of a suspect's well-preserved genes, when it's clear how that DNA arrived at the crime scene, and when the labs sequencing the sample don't make any mistakes. But there are very few cases in which all of these conditions are met. That means that most DNA evidence presented in courtrooms has some degree of ambiguity to it, which juries may not realize.*[20]

One example of this is the case of Josiah Sutton of Houston, Texas. In 1998, Sutton was identified by a rape victim as one of her attackers, even though he did not fit the suspect's description. He willingly submitted to a DNA test, believing that since he had not committed the crime, there was no way the DNA could match. He was shocked when the DNA showed that his blood matched the semen taken from the backseat of the victim's car. This was enough to convince a jury to convict Sutton, and he was sentenced to 25 years in jail. However, what the jury did not know at the time was that there were serious problems with the police testing lab in Houston, Texas, where the crime took place. An investigation of the lab found "consistent distortions of the statistical certainty of the DNA evidence … instances that looked like fudging of results, to fit the prosecution's theory of the case. And … a lab that consistently failed to use appropriate scientific procedures."[21] When Sutton's DNA was retested correctly, it was shown not to be

Occupation: Crime Scene Investigator

Job Description:
Crime scene investigators (CSIs) examine a crime scene for evidence, such as hairs, fingerprints, or the presence of hidden blood. They collect this evidence and bring it to a forensics lab for analysis. They also take photographs of the crime scene and note anything that seems unusual.

Education:
The type of education needed depends on the place that is offering the job. Some positions require only a high school diploma, but most require a bachelor's of science (BS) degree in forensic science, forensic anthropology, biology, or chemistry. People who do not have a BS in forensic science may be required to take additional courses to earn what is called a certificate. Certificate courses teach people about a specific topic but take less time to complete than a degree.

Qualifications:
Being a CSI requires extreme attention to detail; they must be able to spot small items such as hairs and figure out which parts of a crime scene are the most important—something that is not always obvious. They must also have strong problem-solving and organizational skills, and they must not be bothered by blood, dead bodies, and other graphic scenes.

Salary:
The average salary of a crime scene investigator is between $34,000 and $94,400.

a match, and he was released in 2003.

In October 2017, *Last Week Tonight with John Oliver* aired a segment about how errors in forensic science are more common than people realize. Although experts do their best to match the evidence at a crime scene with the correct person, sometimes mistakes happen; however, people are so used to thinking of forensic evidence—including DNA—as foolproof that they may unintentionally convict an innocent person. Forensic expert Brad Hart, director of the Lawrence Livermore National Laboratory (LLNL) Forensic Science Center, pointed out that often DNA from multiple sources can be found at a crime scene. For instance, there may be more than one victim or more than one perpetrator, and their blood or other DNA sources may be mixed together. Additionally, DNA is fragile and breaks down easily. All of these factors make getting a 100 percent positive match nearly impossible. In one case, a lawyer told a jury that "the odds the defendant's DNA matched the glove found at the scene by chance was 1 in 1.1 billion … but it turned out the glove actually contained at least three people's DNA and a later analysis put the odds closer to 1 in 2."[22]

Another little-known problem is the fact that the police who work with lab technicians may unconsciously develop a bias toward a particular suspect based on early, unproven lab results. Jennifer Mnookin of the UCLA School of Law explained that some police officers develop a bias because they want to feel as if they are "part of a team … and … want to get the bad guy."[23] This can lead to law enforcement officials going after the wrong person, even if later DNA results prove that person's innocence.

Some laws have been proposed to try to combat these problems. For example, Texas recently passed a law allowing convicts to request a new trial if the forensic science that resulted in their conviction was not done well. Federal laws were proposed, but the commission overseeing those laws was shut down in

April 2017 by Attorney General Jeff Sessions. This means it is now up to the states to make those kinds of laws, which can be a slow process. In the meantime, individuals who are called to jury duty can help by educating themselves on the way the forensic process actually works and looking at DNA and other types of forensic evidence skeptically.

DNA Evidence versus Eyewitness Accounts

As cases involving DNA profiling go, those of Tommie Lee Andrews and Sarah Johnson were fairly uncomplicated. The police had suspicions that a certain person was guilty, and the DNA evidence confirmed those suspicions. However, sometimes DNA evidence proves police suspicions wrong, even when there is a strong case against a suspect, such as eyewitness accounts. For example, in 1984, five eyewitnesses testified that Kirk Bloodsworth had murdered a nine-year-old girl. He was sentenced to death, but nine years later, DNA testing proved him innocent, and he was released before the death sentence could be carried out. How was this possible when five people could testify to him committing the crime?

This can happen in part because eyewitness accounts—statements given by people who were involved with a crime, such as the victim, or who saw it happen—are largely unreliable. Witnesses may not be lying, but because of the way human memory works, their accounts may still be wrong. Often, eyewitnesses will believe what they are saying but have misremembered an incident or have been subconsciously swayed to believe that they remember something they do not. A lot of research has been done to explain why this happens; respected memory researcher and psychologist Elizabeth F. Loftus explained that although people tend to think of their memories as unchangeable recordings, that is not actually the case. She compared the act of remembering more to putting together a puzzle than watching a video: "Even questioning by a lawyer can alter the witness's testimony because fragments of the memory may be unknowingly combined with information provided by the questioner, leading to inaccurate recall."[24]

In fact, many things can cause an eyewitness account to be inaccurate. These include extreme stress during the crime or during testimony; disguises (even bad ones); too-brief viewing during

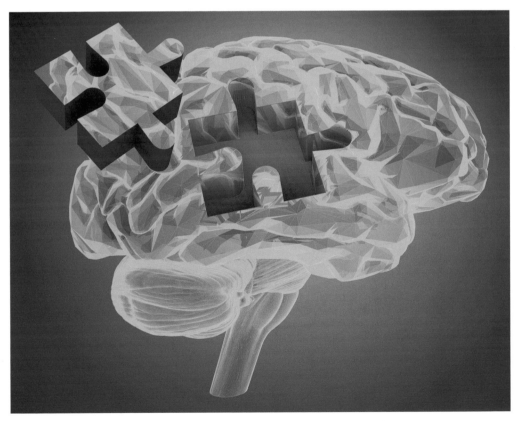

Memories are less like recordings and more like puzzles.

identification procedures; a lack of distinct features on the suspect, such as tattoos or other notable characteristics; and a conscious or unconscious bias, such as a difference in race between the witness and the suspect. Such differences may account for part of why so many exonerations due to DNA evidence are of racial minorities: As of 2016, 61 percent of exonerated individuals were non-white.

Warming Up a Cold Case

Often, DNA evidence can be used immediately to convict the perpetrator of a crime. However, two features of DNA evidence—that DNA can last a long time and that forensics labs freeze DNA samples for future reference—provide law enforcement with the ability to solve crimes many years after they occur. In this way, police are able to reopen and solve more cold cases than they could in the past.

Indeed, similar to the Rodney J. Crooks case in Cincinnati, many seemingly unsolvable cold cases have been resolved thanks to state databases of prison inmates' DNA information. DNA evidence from cold crimes can then be compared to these prisoners' DNA profiles. Some states have shown extremely encouraging results. For example, Gary Stone, an officer in the Texas Department of Public Safety,

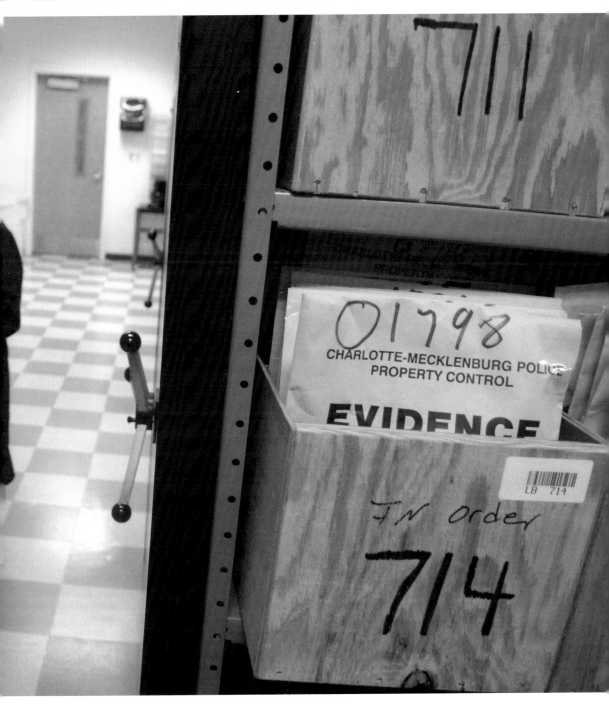

Cold cases can go unsolved for years, but DNA evidence has allowed police to find new evidence with which to prosecute.

reported, "We are having some phenomenal results on cases that would have never been solved and people who would have never been arrested. It is unbelievable how far we've come, but also how far we can go."[25]

Law enforcement officials in the state of Washington have also scored successes using DNA to solve cold cases in recent years. One of the most stunning was that of a young singer named Mia Zapata, who was raped and murdered in Seattle, Washington, in 1993. Police investigators were at first baffled by the crime. The only evidence they were able to find consisted of some small drops of saliva on Zapata's chest. The sample was too small to analyze with the RFLP method, which was the only DNA test available to the local forensics lab at the time. As a result, months and years went by and the case grew colder and colder. At one point, the victim's disappointed father, Richard Zapata, remarked, "I could live and die, and this murder could remain unsolved."[26]

Even after STR technology became available, police could not find a match. However, in December 2002, the saliva found at the murder scene was found to be a match to Jesus Mezquia, who was living in Florida by then. This shows the limitations of the DNA databases: They only contain the DNA of people who have already been convicted of a crime. When police tried running the DNA in 2001, they did not come up with a match because Mezquia had not been convicted of a crime at that time. When they tried again in 2002, Mezquia had been arrested for burglary and domestic abuse, so his DNA was in the database. Mezquia was arrested in January 2003 and stood trial in Washington, where he was convicted and sentenced to 36 years in prison.

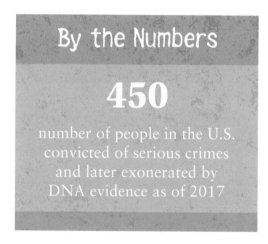

By the Numbers

450

number of people in the U.S. convicted of serious crimes and later exonerated by DNA evidence as of 2017

Evidence and Exoneration

Few exoneration cases have been more riveting that of Gary Dotson. A resident of Chicago's suburbs, Dotson was the first American ever exonerated by DNA evidence.

Dotson's nightmare began in July 1977, when he was 22. On July 9, a 16-year-old girl named Cathleen Crowell told police that she had just been abducted and raped. Three young men had forced her into their car, she said, and one had raped her in the back seat. "I tried to fight him off," she later testified, "and I couldn't."[27] Crowell aided a police artist in preparing a sketch of the alleged rapist. Soon afterward, she positively identified Dotson, both from his picture in a mug book (a collection of photos of criminal suspects) and in a lineup. Dotson insisted that he was not guilty. Also, at the time of his arrest, he had a mustache that he could not have grown in less than a month. Despite the fact that Crowell's sketch was of a clean-shaven man, the authorities ignored this piece of evidence and charged Dotson with the crime. He was tried, found guilty, and sentenced to 25 to 50 years in jail.

Later, Crowell got married and moved to New Hampshire. One day in 1985, she told her pastor that she was wracked with guilt because years before, she had falsely accused a man of rape and that the man was still suffering in prison. Crowell explained that back in 1977, she was worried that she might be pregnant with her boyfriend's baby and was afraid her parents might punish her, so she made up the rape charge. Furthermore, even when she found that she was not pregnant, she continued to lie; by that time, she was too scared of the consequences to tell the truth.

However, Dotson's conviction was only partially Crowell's fault. If law enforcement had properly investigated the case, the evidence should have proved his innocence. In addition to ignoring important evidence such as Dotson's facial hair, mistakes were made in analyzing some of the evidence. The Innocence Project described just one of several mistakes:

> *A forensic analyst testified that he examined semen on the victim's undergarments and found evidence of blood groups A and B. Both Dotson and the victim had type B blood. The analyst incorrectly [testified] that Dotson could have been the source of the semen, despite the evidence of type A blood that should have excluded him.*[28]

Even after Crowell confessed, the governor of Illinois refused to pardon Dotson because he did not believe Crowell's confession. It was not until August 1988 that a DNA profile finally cleared Dotson, and it was another year before a motion was made to end the conviction. Dotson's lawyers did not know such technology existed until 1987, and they had to wage long legal battles before the court approved the test. The DNA analysis proved that he was innocent and that Cathleen Crowell had told her pastor the truth about her false accusation. "It's been 12 long grueling years," Dotson told reporters after his exoneration. "I'm

Gary Dotson (tan shirt) spent years in prison after being falsely accused of rape and repeatedly denied a DNA test.

An Activist's Struggle

Kirk Bloodsworth, who was wrongfully convicted of murder in 1985 and later exonerated by DNA analysis, has become an important voice for people who have been wrongly imprisoned. He speaks out frequently against the death penalty, arguing that the chance that a state could put an innocent person to death far outweighs any other considerations. *Washington Post* reporter Susan Levine wrote this emotional account of Bloodsworth's nightmare and how he turned it into a force for positive change:

> *The dream still haunts him, still grabs him in the night and drags him down the long hallway toward his death. He always fights back, kicking at the faceless guards forcing him on, but there is no escape. The metal-studded gas chamber looms ... And then ... Kirk Bloodsworth wakes up, drenched in terror, choking to breathe ... "It's a daily struggle," Bloodsworth says. "You're fighting with the fact you went through this." For the longest time, he wouldn't talk about the past. Ignoring it was the way to move on. But these days, his is one of the most prominent voices within the small, exclusive club of death-row exonerees ... Bloodsworth addresses legislative committees, legal conferences and university students ... and argues against capital punishment for the most fundamental of reasons. "As long as there's the possibility—no matter how remote— that an innocent person could be killed," he says, "nobody should be for the death penalty."*[1]

1. Susan Levine, "Maryland Man's Exoneration Didn't End Nightmare," *Washington Post*, February 24, 2003. www.washingtonpost.com/archive/politics/2003/02/24/md-mans-exoneration-didnt-end-nightmare/9f426085-7344-4614-b399-bb5d29696418/?utm_term=.b9022b1ae9b1.

relieved it's over ... [But] the stigma remains. It's something I have to deal with. I've been referred to as a 'convicted rapist.' Now, at least, I'm no longer 'convicted'."[29]

This case, obviously traumatic and devastating for Dotson, did double harm: It reinforced the narrative of the false rape accusation. Only about 2 percent of all rape and related sex charges are false; in fact, it is much more common for a woman not to accuse her attacker at all. Psychological trauma, the stigma of being at the center of a sexual assault trial, fear of not being believed, the traumatic experience of undergoing the rape kit exam, and the grim reality that only half of sexual assault reports lead to prosecution cause many women not to come forward after an assault takes place.

Cruel and Unusual

The death penalty is deeply controversial in the United States. It is legal in 31 states, but very few states perform it often; in fact, the number of prisoners executed every year has been steadily declining since 1999, when a total of 98 people were executed in the United States. By 2016, that number had dropped to 20.

There were 159 exonerations of prisoners on death row in the United States by mid-2017; in 30 percent of them, DNA evidence played a substantial role. The first death row inmate in the world exonerated this way was Kirk Bloodsworth of Cambridge, Maryland. His harrowing story has received a great deal of media attention over the years.

In 1984, Bloodsworth, then 24, was accused of raping and killing a 9-year-old girl. The evidence against him was all circumstantial, which means law enforcement officials could not prove conclusively whether or not he was guilty. First, he lived and worked in the general area of the crime. Second, two boys said they saw him walking near the crime scene on the day it occurred. These two facts are considered circumstantial evidence because they did not prove that he had committed the crime, only that he had an opportunity to do so. The only forensic evidence at the crime scene was a small semen stain on the girl's underwear, which at that time could not be matched to Bloodsworth because DNA analysis did not yet exist. Still, the jury found him guilty. This was partly because the prosecutors in the case believed he was the murderer and argued his guilt in court. "The more I got involved in preparing for the case," stated one of the prosecutors, Robert Lazzaro, "the more convinced I was that we had the right guy ... In my mind, he testified and acted consistent with someone who (was guilty). He didn't act like someone who was unjustly accused ... I never would have prosecuted a case I didn't believe in."[30]

However, even though the prosecution and jury thought Bloodsworth was guilty, he kept insisting he was innocent all through his nine years in prison, two of which were spent on death row.

Fortunately for Bloodsworth, while he was waiting for his death sentence to be carried out, DNA profiling technology was becoming a standard practice in the U.S. criminal justice system. Before the state of Maryland was able to execute him, his lawyer secured him a DNA test. It showed conclusively that his DNA did not match that in the semen found on the victim. The court immediately released Bloodsworth and the state paid him $330,000 in an attempt to make up for his wrongful imprisonment.

As for Bloodsworth's life since his exoneration, he works as a fisherman and also gives lectures across the country.

The death penalty is hotly debated in the United States, and the number of executions has been dramatically reduced in recent years.

He promotes various reforms of the justice system. In particular, he urges more use of DNA testing to free people wrongly convicted of crimes. "Did the system work?" he asked one audience:

I was released, but only after eight years, eleven months, and nineteen days, all that time not knowing whether I would be executed ... My life has been taken from me and destroyed. I was separated from my family and branded the worst thing possible—a child killer.[31]

Despite his bitterness over his terrible ordeal, Bloodsworth realized that, in one way, he was fortunate. He received his DNA test in time to preserve his life. Not all death row inmates are so lucky. For example, Florida man Frank Lee Smith spent 14 years on death row for a murder he said he did not commit. His lawyers asked repeatedly that he be

By the Numbers

11.3

average number of years between a wrongly accused person being sentenced to death and exonerated

allowed to have a DNA test, but state prosecutors blocked it. Smith finally had his DNA analyzed in 2000 and the results showed he was innocent, but it was too late. He died of cancer in prison before the state could release him.

Bloodsworth and other advocates of DNA testing say they do not want to see any more cases like Smith's. They argue that the technology must not only be used to find the truth in criminal cases, it must be used with all possible speed.

Chapter Four

Beyond Crime Scenes

Catching and convicting criminals as well as freeing people who have been falsely imprisoned are among the most common and important uses for DNA testing techniques. However, today, DNA-related technology is also used in many other ways that are vital in one way or another to science and society at large.

DNA technology gives researchers the ability to see links between people and things they would otherwise have no way of knowing. The genetic code that ties families together, regardless of interpersonal relationships, can help reunite missing children with their families or—less happily—bring closure to loved ones by identifying years-old human remains. Additionally, DNA analysis helps scientists in multiple ways. For example, it can help them trace the migration patterns of human groups over the course of centuries and millennia and even reveal the origins of the human race. In addition, by studying the remains of long dead historical figures, researchers can confirm or disprove how certain key historical deaths and other events occurred.

Lost and Found

Of the many services DNA analysis has come to provide for society, perhaps none is more gratifying and rewarding than reuniting missing children with their families. The most famous case of using DNA forensics in this manner occurred in Argentina, a South American country that experienced a brutal dictatorial regime throughout the 1970s. In an effort to maintain order by spreading fear, leaders of the regime ordered as many as 30,000 innocent people to be tortured, abducted, or killed. Some people simply vanished without a trace; this group of people, whose fates were unknown, is called *los desaparecidos*: the disappeared. Additionally, an estimated

500 babies were abducted from their families and secretly given to high members of the military to raise as their own.

The search for these lost children began after democracy was restored in Argentina in 1983. A group of women known as the Abuelas de Plaza de Mayo (Grandmothers of the Plaza de Mayo) organized to find the children. United States genetic scientist Dr. Mary-Claire King—the scientist who proved that the DNA of humans and chimpanzees is 99 percent identical—has dedicated much of her career to helping the Abuelas in their search. For a long time, these efforts met with very little success. The situation changed dramatically, however, when reliable DNA profiling technology became available in the 1990s. Since that time, human rights groups and other researchers have sponsored many DNA tests. So far, 122 of the missing children

Dr. Mary-Claire King (shown here) has been an essential part of the growth of DNA technology and its application to human rights cases.

World
Science
Festival

World
Science
Festival

Mummies and Egyptian DNA

In 2017, *Business Insider* reported on the results of DNA tests done on Egyptian mummies found at a burial site in Egypt that was dedicated to Osiris, the ancient Egyptian god of death and resurrection:

> *The DNA was extracted from the teeth and bones of mummies … The oldest were from about 1388 BC during the New Kingdom, a high point in ancient Egyptian influence and culture. The most recent were from about 426 AD, centuries after Egypt had become a Roman Empire province.*

> *"There has been much discussion about the genetic ancestry of ancient Egyptians," said archeogeneticist Johannes Krause of the Max Planck Institute for the Science of Human History in Germany, who led the study … "Are modern Egyptians direct descendants of ancient Egyptians? Was there genetic continuity in Egypt through time? Did foreign invaders change the genetic makeup: for example, did Egyptians become more 'European' after Alexander the Great conquered Egypt? … Ancient DNA can address those questions."*

> *The genomes showed that, unlike modern Egyptians, ancient Egyptians had little to no genetic kinship with sub-Saharan African populations … The closest genetic ties were to the peoples of the ancient Near East, spanning parts of Iraq and Turkey as well as Israel, Jordan, Syria and Lebanon … The researchers found genetic continuity spanning the New Kingdom and Roman times, with the amount of sub-Saharan ancestry increasing substantially about 700 years ago, for unclear reasons.*[1]

1. Will Dunham, "Genetic Tests of Mummies Are Revealing Surprises About the Ancestry of Ancient Egyptians," *Business Insider*, May 31, 2017. www.businessinsider.com/r-whos-your-mummy-genetic-secrets-of-ancient-egypt-un-wrapped-2017-5.

(now adults) have been found. Of these 122, about 30 have been reunited with their biological families, while a few have chosen to stay with their adoptive families or were raised with joint custody. Some of the children identified through DNA tests had died in the intervening years.

King has been working with the Abuelas for decades. Their relationship began in 1984, when King's daughter was the same age the children had been when they went missing. This connection caused King not only to get involved, but to develop new groundbreaking technologies for analyzing genetics using mtDNA. One such case, of Estela de Carlotto—president of the

Abuelas de Plaza de Mayo—spanned decades of searching. In 2014, she was finally reunited with her grandson after DNA sequencing proved their relationship.

By the Numbers

300,000 years

age of the oldest fossil remains of humans, found in Jebel Irhoud, Morocco

Whose Bones Are These?

In addition to tracking down living people, DNA analysis is also routinely used to identify bodies and other human remains. One such example is the extraordinary story of King Richard III of England. Richard III was a controversial figure in his day; when he took power, it was from the hands of his young nephew, Edward V. Rumors circulated that Richard had Edward and Edward's younger brother, who was also named Richard, murdered while they were imprisoned in the Tower of London.

There were two major uprisings against Richard III's rule. The second conflict, led by the Tudor family, killed Richard III at the Battle of Bosworth Field.

Richard III was buried without ceremony, and the site of his remains was a mystery for more than five centuries. In 2012, skeletal remains were discovered beneath a parking lot in Leicester, England. Visual examination of the bones suggested to archaeologists that they might have found Richard III at last—the king was described as having uneven shoulders, and the bones they uncovered showed signs of scoliosis, a bone disorder that could cause this. Additionally, the skeleton showed signs of battle wounds, including a blow to the head that would have been fatal.

However, it would be impossible to know without DNA analysis. Geneticists used mtDNA from two living relatives of Richard, from his mother's side, and compared them to DNA taken from the skeleton. What they found was astounding: Scientists determined "with '99.999 percent' accuracy that the remains of King Richard III of England really were lying under a municipal parking lot."[32]

In another case, DNA was used to identify the remains of Nazi doctor and war criminal Josef Mengele. During World War II, Mengele became notorious for performing cruel medical experiments on living prisoners at Auschwitz, one of the Nazi death camps. After Germany's defeat in the war, Mengele escaped to South America. In 1979, it was reported that he was found drowned in Brazil, but some people were suspicious that he might have faked his death because he was so universally hated. However, in 1992, DNA testing proved that the remains were almost certainly Mengele's.

By the Numbers

6.7 million to 1

the chance that the skeleton found in Leicester is not Richard III

Missing Heirs

When enough viable DNA is recovered from human remains, modern scientists can shed light on well-known historical personalities and events. In some cases, this includes infamous crimes, injustices, or accidents of the past. Though his remains were lost for centuries, there was no doubt as to Richard III's fate; he had been killed on the battlefield. However, not all historical figures have such a clear end.

For example, great mystery surrounds Richard III's nephews—they disappeared completely and were never seen again. Some historians suspect they were murdered on Richard III's orders to strengthen his claim to the throne, but without their remains, it is impossible to say. If these skeletons turn up one day, this mystery may be solved using DNA analysis and other forensic methods. The study of skeletons is the work of specially trained scientists known as forensic anthropologists.

In fact, forensic anthropologists were among the experts who solved two of Europe's greatest royal mysteries: the fates of the French boy-king Louis-Charles and the lost Russian princess, Anastasia.

King Louis XVI and his wife, Marie Antoinette, were executed in 1793, deposed by the French Revolution. This left their eight-year-old son, Louis-Charles, the official king of France—a title which was meaningless in the post-Revolution world, which had ended the monarchy. Officially, according to the revolutionary government, Louis-Charles spent two years in a windowless cell in a Paris prison before dying of tuberculosis in June 1795 at age 10. However, many people in France and elsewhere did not believe this claim, viewing it as a cover story created by the new government to make sure the monarchy could never be restored. Australian geneticist Anna Meyer described the mystery and rumors surrounding Louis-Charles:

Almost immediately, people began to whisper that Louis-Charles was not dead—that the prince had been exchanged at some earlier time for another child, who had died in his place. The real Louis XVII was [rumored to be] hidden somewhere, most likely away from France. There was absolutely no proof that the child who died was the genuine Louis-Charles ... Even the warders who had guarded him could neither confirm nor deny whether the child who died was the real Louis XVII ... To add to the mystery, no one who knew him as a young child, not even his sister, had been permitted to identify the body.[33]

For nearly two centuries, historians and others argued over whether Louis-Charles had died in prison or had survived into adulthood. Finally, in the 1990s, various interested parties proposed using the recently introduced DNA profiling technology to settle this argument. To do so, of course, they needed a DNA sample from the child who died in the Paris prison. They also needed a DNA sample from someone related to the French royal family for comparison. No closely related descendants could be found, but a set of rosary beads belonging to Marie Antoinette's mother had survived, and some medallions intertwined with the beads contained locks of hair belonging to Louis-Charles's aunts and uncles.

As for the sample from the imprisoned boy, it so happened that after his death, a doctor had removed and saved his heart in a jar. Modern investigators managed to find the heart; forensic scientists went to work and were able to confirm conclusively that the boy who died in the prison was indeed the crown prince. Thanks to DNA analysis, the mystery had at last been solved.

Much like Louis-Charles, Anastasia Romanov was the child of a deposed monarch: Nicholas II, the last Czar of Russia, and his wife Alexandra. The family was exiled to Yekaterinburg, Russia, after Nicholas II gave up his throne during the Russian Revolution, ending the 300-year reign of the Romanov family in Russia. Nicholas II; Alexandra; their only son, Alexei; and their four daughters, Tatiana, Olga, Maria, and Anastasia, were held by Ural Soviet forces in exile, along with some members of their staff. Then, in the still-dark morning of July 17, 1918, they were executed by firing squad.

Nicholas II and his family were the last of the Romanovs, a family that had ruled Russia for 300 years.

However, as with Louis-Charles, rumors about the family's true fate spread. For almost 90 years, the Soviet government denied their deaths; rumors persisted that some members of the family had escaped execution, perhaps due to jewels they had hidden in their clothing. The most popular of these rumors was that Anastasia Romanov, the youngest daughter, had avoided death. This doubt allowed for a flood of individuals claiming to belong to the Romanov family—since 1918, more than 200 people made this assertion. The most famous case is that of Anna Anderson, who convinced many people that she was indeed Anastasia, including some close friends of the Romanov family. Even the courts could not say definitively whether or not she was lying; a lawsuit against her ended without reaching a conclusion. She looked like Anastasia, had similar scars and similar

The Last Czar of Russia

When modern researchers examined the supposed remains of the last Russian Czar, Nicholas II, the first DNA test they performed was inconclusive. The investigators managed to find two living descendants of the Romanovs, the royal family to which Nicholas belonged. They compared the mtDNA from these relatives to the mtDNA found in the decades-old remains. Though the genetic material in all three samples was very similar, the mtDNA from the remains did not exactly match that from the living relatives. The researchers suspected that Nicholas had a very rare condition known as heteroplasmy, which is the presence of multiple types of mtDNA in the same cell. To test this theory, the investigators obtained permission to exhume the body of Nicholas's brother, Georgij Romanov. Sure enough, Georgij's mtDNA had the same odd heteroplasmy markers as Nicholas's did. The perfect match showed that the remains were indeed those of Nicholas and that the heteroplasmy had disappeared in later generations of Romanovs.

mannerisms, recognized music that had been written for the Romanov children, and had nearly identical handwriting. In 1997, an animated movie called *Anastasia* was made that followed this basic plot, although the creators added some historically inaccurate details.

Even the exhumation (digging up) of a mass grave by a local geologist named Dr. Alexander Avdonin did not stop the rumors. The grave was discovered in 1970, but out of fear of the Soviet government's reaction, Avdonin kept it a secret until the fall of the Soviet Union in 1991. The forensic analysis of the bodies in the grave revealed that death had not been easy. Nicholas II was shot; his daughters were killed by bayonet, then burned, then doused in acid and buried in an attempt to make sure the bodies were never found. However, two of the Romanov children—Alexei and one of his sisters, thought to be either Maria or Anastasia—were missing from the 1991 exhumation. Digs around the area, searching for the lost remains, turned up nothing. Some people thought it was still possible, after everything, that Alexei and one of the girls had escaped. Could it be that Anna Anderson had been telling the truth all along? Was she indeed the lost child?

Then, in 2007, a Russian builder named Sergei Plotnikov was digging a hole when he hit bone with his shovel.

Forensic anthropologists examined the remains and tested their DNA; it was a 10- to 13-year-old boy and an 18- to 23-year-old woman. DNA testing confirmed they were the bodies of the missing Romanovs. Whether it is Maria or Anastasia buried with Alexei is impossible to say, but the tests conclusively determined that none of the Romanovs survived. DNA tests performed on parts of Anna Anderson's body after her death in 1984 confirmed that she was most likely not a Romanov, but in fact a Polish woman named Franziska Schanzkowska. However, the mystery of how she knew so much about Anastasia's past, as well as how she looked and acted so much like her, was never solved.

The Origins of the Species

The same technology that solved royal mysteries and returned lost children to their families promises to answer far older questions as well. Because DNA can, under favorable circumstances, last for many thousands of years, DNA analysis is beginning to reveal secrets about Stone Age humans, their migrations, and even the origins of modern humanity.

For example, recent studies of the DNA of modern humans suggest that all people alive today are, genetically speaking, nearly identical. Among other things, these studies looked at average rates of mutations, or natural changes in the human genome, and traced these changes backward in time. The studies found the startling fact that all humans, no matter where in the world they are from, have nearly identical DNA.

This analysis of modern human DNA indicates that a common ancestor lived about 200,000 years ago, but this is not an exact estimate; because of the problems with testing older DNA, she may actually have lived anywhere from 50,000 to 500,000 years ago. That ancestor was one of a small group of early humans who were descended from still older humans. The same studies suggest that this common human ancestral group originated in Africa.

Researchers have nicknamed humanity's common ancestor Mitochondrial Eve because her mtDNA is in everyone. The website HowStuffWorks explained how it is possible for humanity to all be descended from one woman:

The likeliest possibility is that an evolutionary bottleneck occurred among humankind while Eve was alive. This is a situation where a large majority of the members of species suddenly die out, bringing the species to the verge of extinction ... Afterward, just a few members remain to repopulate the group and continue to evolve … If the human population was reduced dramatically, and there weren't many women around to have kids, the stage is set for one "Lucky Mother" … to emerge as a most recent common ancestor. It's possible that after a few generations, the mtDNA of the other women died out. If a woman produces only male offspring, her mtDNA won't be passed along, since children don't receive mtDNA from their father. This means that while the woman's sons will have her mtDNA, her grandchildren won't, and her line will be lost.[34]

Reuniting separated families, unraveling historical mysteries, and searching for humanity's origins are only a few of the many ingenious uses devised for DNA technology in recent years. Experts agree that the technology is still in its infancy, so it is likely that future uses will be developed that people today have not yet imagined.

Chapter Five
A Darker Side of DNA

No one argues that DNA profiling technology has not revolutionized the criminal justice system in recent years. DNA analysis can be a powerful tool for law enforcement to uncover guilty parties in criminal cases and to free individuals who have been falsely accused and imprisoned.

However, DNA databases and DNA analysis can be a double-edged sword. Like any other powerful technology, it has the potential for misuse or unintended negative consequences. Issues such as the planting of DNA samples at crime scenes for police to find, the disproportionate policing of certain neighborhoods, and a fundamental misunderstanding of what DNA reveals are a sobering reminder that, like all advances in crime-solving and technology, DNA is not magic and there are no easy answers.

Who Does DNA Belong To?

Among these potential negative consequences, perhaps the most widely debated issue is personal privacy. A number of critics say DNA testing is already being used to invade people's privacy through its ability to reveal intimate details about them. Additionally, DNA is often so individual-specific that even a profile without names or other identifiers can lead back to the person who supplied the DNA sample. This can affect more than just one person:

> *Research subjects who share their DNA may risk a loss of not just their own privacy but also that of their children and grandchildren, who will inherit many of the same genes, said Mark B. Gerstein, a Yale professor who studies large genetic databases ... Even fragments of genetic information can compromise privacy.*[35]

*DNA databases have made people question
what rights to genetic privacy they have.*

This fear of the power of genetic fingerprinting to intrude into and lay bare people's personal lives is not limited to members of the media or any other single societal group. It is shared by all kinds of people, including the scientists who developed or continue to use the technology. DNA can tell researchers a lot about people and their families, including which diseases they are likely to develop, whether they are adopted, and other private information. Some people fear that if this information is made available to the government, insurance companies, employers, schools, and other agencies, DNA may be used to discriminate against people.

Of these potential discriminators, insurers have frequently been singled out in recent years. Many critics say that insurance companies have particularly strong incentives for possible misuse of information taken from DNA testing. The fear is that some of these companies may discriminate against clients whose DNA profiles show that they have a high likelihood of developing serious health problems later. This, critics say, would significantly reduce costs for insurers, but at the expense of individuals who would no longer be able to afford health care. At the same time, it would raise both legal and ethical red flags, raising questions about possible infringements on a client's civil rights. One effect of the Affordable Care Act (ACA), which was passed in 2010, was to ban insurance companies from denying people health insurance based on pre-existing conditions. Some people hope the ACA will be repealed because they believe it does more harm than good; others support the effects of the act. The Council for Responsible Genetics, a nonprofit organization located in Cambridge, Massachusetts, did not specifically state whether it was for or against the act, but it did make a statement regarding the potential danger of allowing health insurance companies to deny insurance to people based on their genes:

Whereas individuals can exercise choices about whether to smoke, how much exercise they get, and how much fat is in their diets, they cannot change the contents of their genes. To make employment or insurance decisions on the basis of genetic characteristics determined at the moment of conception is to discard cherished beliefs in justice and equality.[36]

Similar worries have been voiced about the potential for employers, police organizations, government agencies, and other individuals or groups to misuse DNA information.

These worries have led to debates among lawmakers on local, state, and federal levels. In fact, several U.S. states have already passed legislation that prohibits insurance companies, the police, employers, and others from some types of genetic discrimination. In 2008, the federal government passed the Genetic Information Nondiscrimination Act (GINA), which sought to protect the genetic privacy of the American public. GINA also made it illegal for health insurers or employers to request or require genetic information of an individual or family.

However, a recent push by certain parties to undermine GINA has made inroads against this kind of privacy protection. In 2017, the House Committee on Education and the Workforce passed a bill called the Preserving Employee Wellness Programs Act, which would allow employers to put pressure on employees to participate in DNA testing. Employers seeking to lower their insurance premiums may offer rewards for employees to submit to DNA testing as part of wellness programs. Employees who refuse will either miss out on substantial benefits or possibly even suffer from workplace penalties. This directly undermines GINA and puts the privacy of workers at risk—not to mention their job security.

By the Numbers

654

as of 2017, the number of state-based passed or proposed laws concerning genetic testing in the United States

Racism in DNA Profiling

Another privacy issue related to DNA testing is racial profiling and the possible use of such racial information to discriminate. At present, DNA analysis lacks the ability to identify certain physical characteristics such as skin color. However, the technology can be used to trace a person's ancestry, so if a DNA sample taken from a crime scene reveals African ancestry, the police might assume the suspect has dark skin. Tracing ancestry through DNA is not an exact science and many people with white skin have African DNA, but racism that is ingrained in society may lead police to look exclusively for dark-skinned people. Additionally, critics cite the over-policing of certain neighborhoods as one reason why many more people of color might end up in criminal databases, even if they are not guilty of a crime.

Workplace Discrimination

One of the concerns voiced in recent years about increasingly large DNA databases is that information from these systems might be secretly sold to outside parties, including employers who want to practice discrimination in hiring. This concern is summed up by the Council for Responsible Genetics:

Basing employment decisions on genetic status opens the door to unfounded generalizations about employee performance and increases acceptance of the notion that employers need to exercise such discrimination in order to lower labor costs … [Many] employers face economic pressures to identify workers who are likely to remain healthy. Less absenteeism, reduced life and health insurance costs, and longer returns on investments in employee training all reduce the costs of labor. To the extent that employers believe that genetic information can help identify workers who have a "healthy constitution," they have strong economic incentives to screen applicants and workers.

Such policies victimize all workers. Discrimination against individuals with particular genetic characteristics harms all workers by diverting attention from the need to improve and, if possible, eliminate workplace and environmental conditions that contribute to ill health for everyone.[1]

1. "Genetic Discrimination," Council for Responsible Genetics, accessed September 10, 2017. www.councilforresponsiblegenetics.org/geneticprivacy/DNA_discrim_1.html.

One worry is that, however accurate or inaccurate such racial profiling may be, it might be used to intimidate or persecute an entire racial or ethnic community. Such fears surfaced in Charlottesville, Virginia, in 2003, for example. A serial rapist had been terrorizing the area for several years. A sketch of the suspect was created from eyewitness accounts, and the sketch artist was told that the suspect was black. The local police finally decided to speak to local black men and ask them for DNA samples, a move that ignited both controversy and protests. According to one observer, many in the local black community "saw the DNA sweep, or dragnet, as a form of racial profiling, and an invasion of civil liberties."[37]

Nevertheless, more than 100 African American men in Charlottesville volunteered their DNA in the sweep. Many of them later said that they did so because they felt pressured. This raised another related legal and privacy issue: whether asking for DNA samples from people who are not suspects in a crime can be interpreted as a type of coercion, or intimidation. In other words, a person might fear that refusing to give a sample might make them a suspect and so feel forced to provide the sample. One of the men involved in the Charlottesville sweep explained:

They kept asking, they kept asking. They said since you will not provide a sample, we are going to come to your classes, sit in on them, [and] make sure you really are a student here. I think they're harassing people, they're intimidating people. I think they're obtaining DNA under duress.[38]

The police who conduct such DNA sweeps often argue that their motive is not to harass, but rather simply to catch a criminal. Sometimes, they say, such sweeps are the only means they have of narrowing the search. For instance, Charlottesville's police chief at that time, Tim Longo, gave the following response to charges of DNA racial profiling:

Anything we do in law enforcement is a balance. On one side of the balance scale is [the] need to preserve and protect individual rights. And human dignity. On the other side of the balance scale is the need to perform a legitimate law enforcement purpose. In this case it was to apprehend a serial rapist.[39]

To encourage members of the black community to provide their DNA, Longo made them a deal: People would only have to provide their DNA if there was more evidence of their guilt than their resemblance to the sketch, and if they were proven innocent, their DNA samples would be destroyed rather than kept on file for the police to use in the future.

Some people feel that anything the police need to do to catch a dangerous criminal is justified. Others disagree and feel innocent people's rights need to be protected even if it makes it harder for police to find a suspect. This argument has been ongoing for many years and will likely continue for the foreseeable future.

The Double-Edged Database

Another mounting legal and ethical concern involves the relationship between rapidly advancing DNA technology and existing DNA databases. Some people worry that technological advances will sooner or later make these databases obsolete, or at least less efficient. When that happens, the critics warn, it could create legal

DNA and Science Fiction

Since it has become known what DNA analysis can do, many books, movies, and television shows have featured unethical, sometimes futuristic uses for the technology. These include *Jurassic Park*, in which dinosaurs are cloned with disastrous results; *The Island of Doctor Moreau*, in which a mad scientist combines human and animal DNA; and *Gattaca*, which focuses on many of the fears people have about DNA analysis.

Gattaca is set in a futuristic society where every person's DNA is sequenced the moment they are born. This information determines everything about a person's life, including what kind of job they can have. The protagonist of the movie, Vincent, has always dreamed of being an astronaut in the Gattaca space program, but his DNA is considered inferior, so he cannot be accepted. In desperation, he makes a deal with a man named Jerome. Using Jerome's superior DNA, Vincent takes on his identity, but at great personal risk. This movie highlights what many people fear could happen if employers, government agencies, and others were allowed unlimited access to a person's DNA.

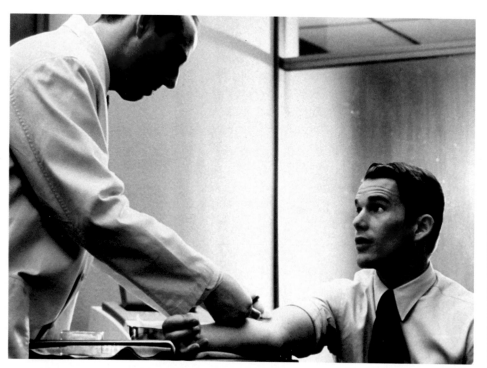

In Gattaca, *Ethan Hawke (right) plays Vincent, a man whose DNA prevents him from getting the job he has always dreamed of.*

challenges to DNA profile matches obtained from such systems. Even Sir Alec Jeffreys has expressed concerns about outmoded databases. "To pretend that we've gone from [the system I introduced] to the ultimate DNA typing system is nonsense," he stated:

There'll be other ones coming along [even more advanced than PCR and STR], and that actually creates a major problem for the forensic scientist who is interested in databasing, because once you go in for very large-scale databasing of many thousands of people— you are trapped in that technology. You cannot change that technology because you've got to retype everybody in the database if you do. So the drive towards databasing, I think, is in fundamental conflict with the still rapidly evolving field of forensic DNA typing—the technology itself.[40]

Databases have the potential to do as much harm as they do good. In 2000, police in Manchester, England, collected some biological evidence at the site of a burglary. The local forensics lab analyzed the sample using a version of the STR method that recognized six loci, or gene locations (each containing several tandem repeats), on a DNA molecule. The odds of the genetic information in all 6 loci being identical in 2 separate individuals were about 1 in 37 million. They then entered the profile into England's national DNA database, which at the time, contained about 660,000 DNA profiles. Because that number is so much smaller than 37 million, the analysts assumed there would be little chance of a random match. When a match was found, the police promptly arrested the man whose DNA in the database matched that found at the crime scene.

However, the suspect strongly insisted he was innocent. Moreover, he had proof that he was somewhere else when the crime occurred. Nevertheless, based on the strength of the DNA match alone, he was kept in jail for months awaiting trial. Fortunately for him, his attorney demanded that a second, more comprehensive DNA test be performed. This time the analysts compared the genetic information in nine loci rather than six, raising the odds of a random match to one in many billions. Sure enough, the suspect's DNA no longer matched that found at the crime scene.

Clearly, the database match had been random and false—an improbably unlucky coincidence. The culprit and suspect were among a handful of people in the world whose DNA matched in six genetic locations.

DNA *analysis is performed by humans and is therefore just as subject to human error as any other process.*

Only when a higher number of loci were considered did the uniqueness of their individual DNA profiles become apparent. Forensic DNA experts Rudin and Inman explained the implications and lessons of this now famous case:

> *It is not only unsurprising, but expected, that the larger the database, the greater chance of a coincidental match. As databases grow, greater numbers of ... loci are required to reduce the possibility of an [accidental] hit ... Additionally, a profile frequency of one in 37 million does not mean that the six loci cannot match more than one person in 37 million ... It does not mean that there cannot be two [such matches], and it also does not exclude the possibility of finding two of the same six-locus profiles in the first 660,000 people tested.*[41]

DNA testing can also be mangled or misread by the people performing it. There are so many ways for DNA samples to be mishandled, contaminated, or simply misunderstood. Multiple cases have shown that DNA evidence, while certainly a useful tool in crime solving, cannot be the only piece of the puzzle and must be treated with the same skepticism as all other evidence. The fact that many people simply accept DNA findings without examination is a large concern for critics. According to *The Atlantic*,

> *DNA typing has long been held up as the exception to the rule— an infallible technique rooted in unassailable science. Unlike most other forensic techniques, developed or commissioned by police departments, this one arose from an academic discipline, and has been studied and validated by researchers around the world ... The problem, as a growing number of academics see it, is that science is only as reliable as the manner in which we use it—and in the case of DNA, the manner in which we use it is evolving rapidly.*[42]

New York University (NYU) law professor Erin Murphy added,

> *Ironically, you have a technology that was meant to help eliminate subjectivity in forensics ... But when you start to drill down deeper into the way crime laboratories operate today, you see that the subjectivity is still there: Standards vary, training levels vary, quality varies.*[43]

In other words, DNA testing is just as subject to human error as any other technology used by humans.

Looking Ahead

There are two sides to the DNA analysis coin. On the one hand, DNA analysis and profiling has the potential to do much good: reuniting families, solving mysteries, exonerating the falsely accused, and catching criminals. On the other, like all techniques managed by humans, it is subject to human error and bias. Both the process of DNA testing and the collection of DNA profiles are the source of ethical arguments and legal disputes, along with privacy, racial profiling, and other issues relating to people's civil rights.

When it comes to DNA, there are no easy answers. It is tempting to treat the technology as a foolproof solution, but it is not. As the technology moves forward—which it certainly will—it is vital that all parties treat DNA technology as what it is: a useful but sometimes flawed tool to help shed light on potential answers, not final answers. There are always more questions to be asked.

Notes

Introduction:
Crime Scene Science

1. Quoted in E.J. Wagner, *The Science of Sherlock Holmes.* New York, NY: John Wiley, 2006, p. 8.
2. Quoted in Wagner, *Science of Sherlock Holmes*, p. 8.
3. Robin Franzen, "TV's 'CSI' Crime Drama Makes It Look Too Easy," *Portland Oregonian*, December 10, 2002.
4. Harlan Levy, *And the Blood Cried Out: A Prosecutor's Spellbinding Account of the Power of DNA.* New York, NY: HarperCollins, 1996, p. 199.

Chapter One:
The Early Days of DNA

5. "Observable Human Characteristics," Learn.Genetics, accessed August 30, 2017. learn.genetics.utah.edu/content/basics/observable/.
6. Quoted in "Sir Alec Jeffreys Discusses Developments in DNA Fingerprinting," The Lister Institute of Preventative Medicine, accessed September 1, 2017. www.lister-institute.org.uk/institute-news/slider-post-1/.
7. Quoted in Graeme Donald, *The Accidental Scientist: The Role of Chance and Luck in Scientific Discovery.* London, UK: Michael O'Mara Books Limited, 2013, e-book.
8. Quoted in "Sir Alec Jeffreys on DNA Profiling," Science Watch. www.sciencewatch.com/interviews/sir_alec_jeffreys.htm.
9. Levy, *And the Blood Cried Out*, p. 25.
10. Ngaire E. Genge, *The Forensic Casebook: The Science of Crime Scene Investigation.* New York, NY: Ballantine, 2002, p. 144.
11. Quoted in Steven Monroe Lipkin and Jon R. Luoma, *The Age of Genomes: Tales from the Front Lines of Genetic Medicine.* Boston, MA: Beacon Press, 2016, p. 176.
12. Levy, *And the Blood Cried Out*, p. 31.

Chapter Two:
How to Build a DNA Profile

13. Quoted in Genge, *Forensic Casebook*, p. 146.
14. Genge, *Forensic Casebook*, p. 149.
15. Norah Rudin and Keith Inman, *An Introduction to Forensic DNA Analysis.* New York, NY: CRC, 2002, p. 16.

16. Kristine Wadosky, e-mail interview by author, August 29, 2017.

17. Genge, *Forensic Casebook*, p. 151.

18. "Combined DNA Index System (CODIS), FBI.gov, accessed September 29, 2017. www.fbi.gov/services/laboratory/biometric-analysis/codis.

Chapter Three: A Brief History of DNA Profiling

19. Quoted in "Expert: Daughter's DNA Found on Evidence at Slain Parents' Home," CNN.com, February 18, 2005. www.cnn.com/2005/LAW/02/18/johnson/index.html.

20. Alexandra Ossola, "DNA Evidence Is Not Foolproof," *Popular Science*, June 25, 2015. www.popsci.com/dna-evidence-not-foolproof.

21. Quoted in Rebecca Leung, "DNA Testing: Foolproof?," *60 Minutes*, May 27, 2003. www.cbsnews.com/news/dna-testing-foolproof/.

22. "Forensic Science: *Last Week Tonight with John Oliver* (HBO)," YouTube video, 18:50, posted by LastWeekTonight, October 1, 2017.

23. "Forensic Science," YouTube video, posted by LastWeekTonight.

24. Quoted in Hal Arkowitz and Scott O. Lilienfeld, "Why Science Tells Us Not to Rely on Eyewitness Accounts," *Scientific American*, January 1, 2010. www.

scientificamerican.com/article/do-the-eyes-have-it/.

25. Quoted in "DNA Cracks Cold Cases," *Austin American-Statesman*, July 24, 2005.

26. Quoted in Rebecca Leung, "Who Murdered the Rock Star?," CBS News, May 14, 2004. www.cbsnews.com/news/who-murdered-the-rock-star-14-05-2004/.

27. Quoted in "The Rape That Wasn't: The First DNA Exoneration in Illinois," Northwestern University Pritzker School of Law, accessed October 2, 2017. www.law.northwestern.edu/legalclinic/wrongful-convictions/exonerations/il/gary-dotson.html.

28. "Gary Dotson," Innocence Project, accessed September 14, 2017. www.innocenceproject.org/cases/gary-dotson/.

29. Quoted in "The Rape That Wasn't."

30. Quoted in Raju Chebium, "Kirk Bloodsworth, Twice Convicted of Rape and Murder, Exonerated by DNA Evidence," CNN, June 20, 2000. edition.cnn.com/2000/LAW/06/20/bloodsworth.profile/.

31. Quoted in Tim Junkin, *Bloodsworth: The True Story of the First Death Row Inmate Exonerated by DNA*. Chapel Hill, NC: Algonquin, 2004, pp. 268–269.

Chapter Four:
Beyond Crime Scenes

32. Lorna Baldwin, "DNA All but Confirms 500-year-old Bones Are King Richard III's," PBS, December 3, 2014. www.pbs.org/newshour/rundown/dna-all-but-confirms-500-year-old-bones-are-king-richard-iiis/.

33. Anna Meyer, *Hunting the Double Helix: How DNA is Solving Puzzles of the Past.* New York, NY: Allen & Unwin, 2005, p. 179.

34. Josh Clark, "Are We All Descended from a Common Female Ancestor," HowStuffWorks, accessed September 14, 2017. science.howstuffworks.com/life/evolution/female-ancestor.htm.

Chapter Five:
A Darker Side of DNA

35. Gina Kolata, "Poking Holes in Genetic Privacy," *New York Times*, June 17, 2013. www.nytimes.com/2013/06/18/science/poking-holes-in-the-privacy-of-dna.html.

36. "Genetic Discrimination," Council for Responsible Genetics, 2001. www.councilforresponsiblegenetics.org/ViewPage.aspx?pageId=85.

37. Quoted in "DNA Testing and Crime," PBS, *Religion & Ethics Newsweekly*, May 28, 2004. www.pbs.org/wnet/religionandethics/week739/cover.html.

38. Quoted in "DNA Testing and Crime."

39. Quoted in "DNA Testing and Crime."

40. Quoted in "Sir Alec Jeffreys on DNA Profiling," Science Watch.

41. Rudin and Inman, *Introduction to Forensic DNA Analysis*, p. 173.

42. Matthew Shaer, "The False Promise of DNA Testing," *The Atlantic*, May 16, 2016. www.theatlantic.com/magazine/archive/2016/06/a-reasonable-doubt/480747/.

43. Quoted in "The False Promise of DNA Testing."

For More Information

Books

Heos, Bridget. *Blood, Bullets, and Bones: The Story of Forensic Science from Sherlock Holmes to DNA*. New York, NY: Balzer + Bray, 2016.
For those interested in the relationship between DNA profiling and criminal justice, this book describes the ever-evolving field of forensic science.

Hunter, William. *DNA Analysis*. Broomall, PA: Mason Crest, 2014.
This book for advanced young readers introduces DNA finger-printing, DNA analysis, and the potential career trajectory of anyone looking to work in applied forensic science.

Kiesbye, Stefan. *DNA Databases*. Detroit, MI: Greenhaven Press, 2012.
Are DNA databases a solution or a complication? Stefan Kiesbye takes a look at the different perspectives on the role of the DNA database in society.

Latta, Sara L. *DNA and Blood: Dead People Do Tell Tales*. Berkeley Heights, NJ: Enslow Publishers, 2012.
Sara Latta looks at real cases in which DNA evidence has been used to solve crimes and reveal dark secrets.

Meyer, Anna. *The DNA Detectives: How the Double Helix Is Solving Puzzles of the Past*. New York, NY: Thunder Mouth, 2005.
Anna Meyer digs into some of history's greatest unsolved puzzles and the way DNA analysis can shed light on mysteries both recent and old.

Wailoo, Keith, Alondra Nelson, and Catherine Lee. *Genetics and the Unsettled Past: The Collision of DNA, Race, and History*. New Brunswick, NJ: Rutgers University Press, 2012.
This book examines the compli-cated intersection between DNA and human history, arguing for a broader approach to the study and understanding of DNA.

Websites

National Human Genome Research Institute (www.genome.gov)
This government website gives the latest information about genetic research.

"How Crime Scene Investigation Works: Analyzing the Evidence" (science.howstuffworks.com/csi5.htm)
HowStuffWorks provides a short but effective overview of the relationship between DNA evidence and crime scene investigations, with a particular emphasis on comparing real CSI investigations to the ones depicted on television.

Learn.Genetics (learn.genetics.utah.edu)
This website, run by the University of Utah, gives easy-to-understand information about all aspects of genetics as well as fun at-home activities.

National Conference of State Legislatures Forensic Laws Database (www.ncsl.org/research/civil-and-criminal-justice/dna-laws-database.aspx)
This website collects all the legislation currently in place regarding DNA and genetics across all 50 U.S. states.

"Pioneering DNA Forensics" (www.npr.org/templates/story/story.php?storyId=4756341)
Read the interview transcript or listen to Sir Alex Jeffreys in conversation with Michele Norris from NPR.

Index

sexual assault evidence kits, 10, 51, 64
Simpson, Orenthal James (O.J.), 12, 53–54
skin cells, 25, 31, 43
Song Ci, 7–8
stigma, 64
Sutton, Josiah, 54

T
Taylor, Alfred Swaine, 8, 10
thymine (T), 14, 19
trace evidence, 25

U
U.S. Department of Justice, 34
U.S. National Institute of Justice, 34

W
Warwick, England, murder in, 8
Watson, James D., 18, 21
workplace discrimination, 86

Z
Zapata, Mia, 60

Picture Credits

About the Author

Cecilia Jennings has always been interested in biology, particularly the study of the human genome and the relationship between health and the environment. She has a degree in food science, which allowed her to explore the field of microbiology, and as a result, she is fascinated by the interaction between the human body and the food it needs. She bakes all her own bread and is currently focused on keeping her sourdough yeast culture alive and thriving. She lives in Wisconsin and works part-time as a cheesemonger, but despite tasting lots of fancy cheeses, her favorite is still Pepper Jack.